COACHED BY THE CURÉ

COACHED BY THE CURÉ

Lessons in Shepherding with St. John Vianney

KEVIN WELLS

Scepter

Copyright © 2025 Kevin Wells

The total or partial reproduction of this book is not permitted, nor its informatic treatment, or the transmission of any form or by any means, including electronic, mechanic, photocopy, or other methods without the prior written permission of the owners of the copyright.

Scripture texts from the Old and New Testaments are taken from The Holy Bible Revised Standard Version Catholic Edition © 1965 and 1966 by the Division of Christian Education of the National Council of Churches of Christ in the United States. All rights reserved. All copyrighted material is used by permission of the copyright owner. No part of it may be reproduced without permission in writing from the copyright owner.

Published by Scepter Publishers, Inc.
info@scepterpublishers.org
www.scepterpublishers.org
800-322-8773
New York
All rights reserved.

Cover Image: John McCoy, Praying with the Saints, oil on canvas, reproduced with permission.
Cover Design: Studio Red Design
Text Design and Pagination: Studio Red Design
Interior Photos: Pages 18, 44, 60, 98, 118: © Fr. Jonathan Meyer, used with permission. Pages 82, 136: © David Taljat, Dreamstime.com. Page 150: Courtesy of Paris Musée under CC0 license.

Paperback ISBN: 978-1-59417-552-7
Ebook ISBN: 978-1-59417-553-4
Library of Congress Control Number: 2024952984

Printed in the United States of America

Contents

This book is dedicated to the hermit Fr. Martin Flum,
who found the cell the Curé never could.

As you will see, the chapters of this book consist of my conception of what St. John Vianney might have thought or said regarding our own time. This imaginative construction is based on his sermons, personal character, biographies, and the historical context of his life. Similarly invented passages from other saints, such as Philomena, are indicated by italics. Statements set within quotation marks are the actual words of Vianney or the other saints.

Foreword

I entered seminary in 1997 and spent seven years in study. Although that seminary was named after the patron saint of all priests—St. John Vianney—he was rarely, if ever, mentioned. The holy saint was not a part of the curriculum or the syllabus. I was never asked to explore or read one of the several biographies written about his life. It was never requested or suggested by formators to study the famous life of the Curé d'Ars, or imitate his virtues, or learn from his soul-saving pastoral approach. Since that time, perhaps this has changed—I am not sure.

Still, all these years later, I find it strange that the man recognized as *the* exemplar for all priests was not spoken of as the foremost model for my priesthood throughout my seminary formation. Abbé François Trochu's acclaimed biography, *The Curé d'Ars: St. John-Marie-Baptiste Vianney*, and the many other books written about Vianney, are mostly read by seminarians in private and in their own time. Sadly, from my lived experience, papal encyclicals and the three letters written by popes on Vianney's saintly life were read "in the dark," in fear that someone might have eavesdropped on a seminarian's desire to live his priesthood as Vianney once did.

There is not a single priest apart from Jesus Christ that has impacted my life as St. John Vianney has. *His life* was my seminary. *He* was my catechist, my priestly model, and the priest I strove to become.

When I began to read Trochu's biography on the Curé in 1999, I could not set it down. A fire began to burn in me. I remember turning the pages of the book and thinking to myself, *Why have I never been urged to read about this priest-saint? Why has John Vianney been hidden from me?* Since then, I've visited Ars, France, seven times; I wrote my master's thesis on his preaching; today I consider St. John Vianney my hero.

I believe this once poor and suffering priest from a tiny French country town in the 1800s is *the answer* to the many issues in the Church and world today. Vianney is the solution and medicine to the hungering souls of today's priests and faithful alike. His life teaches total availability, redemptive suffering, the prioritization of listening, and the uniting of oneself with the Cross. He modeled brave and effective door-to-door evangelization. His refusal to give up or give in, and his industriousness in serving the poor, the orphan, and the rejected are what the world seeks. He preached boldly and effectively. He entered, impacted, and managed to change the lives of countless young people. He radiated joy—and most importantly, he configured his entire life to Jesus and worshiped him each day in the most Blessed Sacrament.

Vianney's entire life is a powerful and necessary lesson for all of today's seminarians and priests. However, he is also a lesson for the rest of us. Aren't we all called to be exemplary in every way that he exuded holiness? Like Vianney, we are called to be great listeners (the man spent fourteen hours a day in the confessional, listening), to be ministers of compassion and mercy (his confessional burned with heaven's grace), to evangelize (he walked to each home in his parish boundary), to focus on the youth (he taught youth catechism every day), to be concerned for those on the peripheries (he opened, funded, and helped to manually build an orphanage for children), to be Eucharistic-focused (he promoted adoration and led processions), to live simply (he gave everything away), to be open to lifelong and nontraditional ways of learning (he was home-schooled by an elderly priest), to be consecrated to Mary (he entrusted every parishioner to Mary, placing their names in a locket around Our Lady's neck). Oh, how this list could go on and on.

John Vianney is a saint for modern times. He died to self and lived, whereas modern man often lives for self and dies. As a priest and pastor of souls, of course he is my patron saint—and laity, too, can glean so much from the holy Curé d'Ars.

Thankfully, Kevin Wells has managed to raise John Vianney from the dead, so to speak, and give voice to the great pastor of souls 166 years after his death in 1859. I first came to know Kevin in 2019, when I was given his book *The Priests We Need to Save the Church.* When I finished reading, I looked him up, made contact, and thanked him for writing a penetrating and encouraging road map to promote holy priesthood. Since then, we've grown in friendship and conversation. Kevin has a heart for priests, for renewal, and for starting fires in people's hearts. In talking to seminarians and priests around the county, I have witnessed how Kevin's words have certainly set hearts ablaze for Christ. His words have brought clarity and hope in the midst of confusion, hurt, and silence.

On a personal level, Kevin has been a blessing to my priesthood. He is a great encourager and coach, and because of his love for people, he works to build them up with hope. God has given him the effective evangelization tools of powerful and captivating wordsmithing and storytelling. The messages in his books draw you in; his words are as alluring as they are convincing. *Coached by the Curé* is yet another page-turning book, much like his previous four.

When Kevin told me about the invitation he'd been given to write *Coached by the Curé*, I was thankful. But when he shared with me that he was going to write the book "with Vianney's tongue" and from his perspective, I grew intrigued. How does one enter into the mind of a deceased saint and speak with his voice? And how would Kevin know how a humble country pastor might address a modern world so very different from the tiny village he once pastored in Ars? Through Kevin's Irish imagination, open heart, and willingness to dive deeply into Vianney's life, he's artfully achieved the task. He has given birth to a poignant, fitting, holy, and encouraging voice by adjusting Vianney's words, coaching, and instruction to open the ears of modern man and penetrate his cacophonous world. The saint speaks directly into it.

I do not know another layman who has more zeal and conviction of Vianney's role as coach for today's world than Kevin. If any writer could have brought Vianney back to life to address the struggles and darkness of our times, it would be Kevin Wells. This is not just a book of solutions to overcoming secularism, materialism, and the sins of modernity; this book comes from the interior stirrings of a fatherly heart.

I believe that the voice of St. John Vianney in *Coached by the Curé* will move the hearts of ordained priests in parishes, but perhaps especially the domestic priests in homes throughout the world. St. John Paul the Great said: "The family is the domestic church. . . . The family is the 'first and vital cell of society.' . . . As the family goes, so goes the nation, and so goes the whole world in which we live."[1] Vianney's witness of sanctity, his conquering over Satan's wiles, his demonstrations of love and sacrifice—*in his own voice*— are sorely needed today in families in the West and beyond. Who better than John Vianney—a man said to have brought more than eighty thousand souls back to the Catholic faith—to reach the fallen-away sons and daughters, aunts and uncles, and, yes, to reach even the hearts of moms and dads, and to love them back into the Church.

My prayer is that Kevin's latest literary effort—through the zeal, power, and loving voice of John Vianney—sparks renewal, conversion, and a return to sanctity in both the Church and in the souls of all believers of Jesus Christ.

Fr. Jonathan Meyer
Pastor of All Saints Parish, St. Lawrence Church, St. Mary's Church, and St. Teresa Benedicta of the Cross Church
Dearborn County, Indiana

1. John Paul II, Homily, Perth, Australia (November 30, 1986). Vatican website: www.vatican.va.

Prologue

Morning sunlight poured through the windows onto the counter of the Crofton, Maryland, library when a woman handed me an on-loan biography of St. John Vianney. *Portrait of a Parish Priest: St. John Vianney, the Curé d'Ars*, written by British author Lancelot Sheppard before World War I, was a small font book with a plain, burnt-orange hardback cover. I remember thinking on that August day in 2018 that the book hadn't been touched since it was written, more than a century earlier.

I left the library and stepped into the shadow of the Catholic Church's summer of shame, in which allegations had been dropping like dull axe swings into the consciences of Catholic laity in the Archdiocese of Washington. Two months earlier, on June 20, the *Washington Post* had laid bare a front-page exposé, detailing then-Cardinal Theodore McCarrick's abuse of a teenage boy in the 1970s. In the days that followed, the Catholic Church was overwhelmed by a flood of revelations that seemed to strike with the fury of Old Testament plagues. A grand jury report out of Pennsylvania indicted the Church for shielding sexually abusive priests for decades. Allegations surfaced of "gay networks" and "lavender mafias" within the clergy. Investigative journalists uncovered scandals in Central and South American seminaries, abuse cases at US parishes, and failures of leadership within the Vatican itself. Perhaps most disheartening of all were reports suggesting that multiple bishops and high-ranking Church officials had known about McCarrick's abuse—and did nothing to stop it.

On a personal level, it was a demoralizing time for those of us, sons and daughters of the Church in Washington, who had grown up in McCarrick's diocese and shared meals with priests around dining room tables. I was friends with quite a few priests—including my brother, Fr. David Wells—who had been ordained by the man now suddenly referred to as "Uncle Ted." Most Washingtonians had regarded McCarrick as a grandfatherly type, well suited to replace the kindly but aging Cardinal James Hickey when he retired in 2000. McCarrick's soft touch and Irish charm softened reporters such as *Meet the Press* host Tim Russert, when he pressed McCarrick on the Molotov cocktails of hidden clergy sin exposed by a team of *Boston Globe* reporters in 2002. Many of the priests had been moved from parish to parish, despite some Boston hierarchy having been aware of their unconscionable offenses.

As the Bride of Christ limped forward in 2003 and 2004, McCarrick was enjoying a meteoric rise in the Church, a trajectory seemingly unchecked. He had gained greater ecclesiastical responsibility and diplomatic weight and had begun to travel the world as a Church ambassador. In time, his decades of sin were made public, and he was laicized on a cold February day in 2019.

Although my parents raised their eight children to see unruly emotions as harmful, that summer my anger at McCarrick, hidden Church sin, and clergy depravity grew in me like an unkillable weed. As a journalist, I both abhorred and applauded what *Washington Post* reporters and other media outlets exposed.

I was not naive to what priestly exceptionalism resembled; it had been revealed to me shortly after leaving the crib. As a young altar boy at St. Pius X Parish in Bowie, Maryland, in the late 1970s and '80s, I was pastored by an Irish-born priest. Fr. Andrew Cassin was one of my first heroes. On certain summers, Fr. Cassin walked door-to-door to every home in our town to invite unsuspecting residents to attend Mass at his parish. If he sensed there was interest, he'd engage his brogue and share warm-hearted stories of growing up in the Irish countryside, gradually shifting the conversation to the meaning of the Eucharist and Sacrifice of the Mass.

An even greater gift, though, was my dad's younger brother, my uncle, Msgr. Thomas Wells. I grew up in the shadow of a man who had been one of the most beloved priests in the Archdiocese of Washington. "Uncle Tommy's" priesthood began at Sacred Heart Parish in my hometown of Bowie, the other parish in town. As a seven-year-old in the 1970s, I used to pedal my little green bike to his parish rectory, located in the heart of a middle-class neighborhood busting at the seams with large young families. As he walked the leafy neighborhood in the early evenings, anxious moms and dads would leave their homes to meet him on the street. There they poured out their concerns over their teenage children growing up in the post-Woodstock generation. There was the bedroom scent of marijuana, a moody daughter's pony-tailed boyfriend, and the new wave of "free love." Over and over, the young new priest calmed their fears by throwing back his head and, in gently mocking laughter, begging them not to worry. If they persisted, he'd howl: "Where is your trust in God in this?!" That single question became one of the hallmark lines of Tom Wells's life. A half century later, virtually all the "hippies" from Bowie are Catholic and have raised their own children in the Faith. How could this be? In part, it was because my uncle entered into the lives of the teenagers. Earning their trust, he gradually channeled their zeal for revolutionary change into a singular devotion to Christ and the sacraments.

I couldn't ask my uncle about McCarrick and the scandals of 2018 because he had been murdered in his parish rectory eighteen years earlier, on June 8, 2000. He would have been seventy-four in 2018, and I imagine as active as ever. But for twenty-nine years he impacted the lives of thousands of Catholic laity in the DC metropolitan area. If he had been alive, though, I know what he would have told me: *Keggy—forget about McCarrick and focus on your family and God's will for you.* Perhaps it was the memory of my uncle's imagined request that slowed the locomotive in my head and gave me the moral clarity that led me to Jean-Marie-Baptiste Vianney. I wanted *to remember again* what Fr. Cassin, Msgr. Wells, and the other faithful priests I knew were like.

So, I began to read about the holy man, and turning the pages of *Portrait of a Parish Priest, St. John Vianney, the Curé d'Ars* became like rotating the cylinder of a kaleidoscope bursting with images of priestly glory. A man barely over five feet seemed taller and more powerful in my imagination than Atlas. Inflamed by love for a spiritually dead village that initially thought him harsh, odd, and overly pious, the curé seemed to bend down to place every soul on his back to get them closer to heaven. Within a short period of time, the country pastor managed to shepherd a mostly faithless and guillotine-haunted village of Ars back to Christ, where they mourned their sin, did penance, and threw themselves on the mercy of God.

Later, tens of thousands of French Catholics and European believers and unbelievers alike took pilgrimages to Ars, where they lined up in seeming formation to lay their eyes on the humble curé and to seek forgiveness for their sins. By the mid-1800s, Vianney was in his confessional for fourteen to sixteen hours every day. Because he loved like Christ, without limit or condition, he absolved more sin than perhaps any priest in the history of the world.

Sheppard's biography was a steady handhold that took me on a pilgrimage far, far away from the summer of shame, escorting me into a graced countryside of order and harmony, where the holy curé seemed to flow from soul to soul as continuously shifting variegated light. I saw, but *God saw, too*, the curé rise from bed around three o'clock each morning at the tolling of the Angelus bell to set out on his well-worn path to his claustrophobic wooden confessional. In the moonglow, he zombied past dozens or a few hundred out-of-town folks who had taken the train to Lyons, then walked forty or so kilometers to Ars, where they slept beneath canopies of walnut trees, waiting to meet the man they had been told could read souls. God *saw* him in his pathetic black shoes, sun-scorched soutane, and weathered breviary tucked beneath his arm, stooping to ruffle an orphan's hair at *La Providence*, the overstuffed village orphanage he paid for and built as a home for God's bullied ones. God *saw* the nightly choruses of demons attempting to blunt his resolve and diminish his priesthood—but God more clearly *saw* the look in Vianney's eyes when the demons tried. God *saw* him standing behind his gothic pulpit and preaching the best he could, despite knowing that keen intellect and theological opulence were not gifts granted to him. And at around eleven o'clock each night, God *saw* him fall bone-tired into bed. But then God saw him often rise again, remembering to reach for *The Lives of the Saints*, the book he cherished, the one he read excerpts from each day of his priesthood. I saw what God saw—moments of inexhaustible love that flickered to life like thousands of fireflies on summer nights—and in those images, my anger fell away.

Ars's curé was more active than Fr. Cassin and more available than my uncle. Biographers believe he worked as many as eighteen hours every day. The centerpiece of Vianney's life was the same as Christ's; he took to the hard wood of the cross and became a victim each day to save souls. He had made a choice early in his priesthood to live uncomfortably, and he keenly understood the fruitfulness of his vocation would be measured by how much of himself he poured out from the cross of his burden to save.

Riding the crest of my emotions the day after finishing Sheppard's book, I wrote an *"Open Letter to Priests."* The article was published on an online Catholic site, which eventually led to my book, *The Priests We Need to Save the Church*. The book was a plea on behalf of Catholic laity for modern-day *curés* at a time when scandals had caused tens of thousands of Catholics to leave the Church. I researched the lives of the greatest priest-saints—John Bosco, Maximilian Kolbe, Philip Neri, John Neumann, Padre Pio, Damien of Molokai, Patrick, and a few others—and laid out eight of the priestly characteristics they shared in common. I also told stories of the Church's modern-day faithful priests and used their witness as unobtrusive reminders of what sacrifice, magnanimity, and virtue did to convert stony, bored, or angry hearts. The book was disseminated into seminaries throughout the world.

It's been seven years since I read *Portrait of a Parish Priest*. Since then, I've read a handful of other biographies of Vianney, as well as letters written about his priesthood by St. John XXIII, St. John Paul II, and Pope Benedict XVI. Since 2018, a first-class relic of Vianney in an old reliquary has sat on my desk, a few feet from me now, as

I type out this sentence. If such things matter to you, I will venerate and pray by his relic each day before writing the book you hold, *Coached by the Curé.*

I imagine in prayer, I'll be asking him these questions: What, Curé, would you prescribe today for a troubled world and a Roman Catholic Church that over the past decade has lost many millions of its once-faithful sons and daughters? How would you encourage today's parents and grandparents to begin to shepherd their fallen-away children back from the grip of Modernism? What measures would you take to inflame our hearts to return to the Sacred Heart of Jesus and to begin to serve God alone? What, Curé, would you do to save this bleeding Church?

How would this holy man respond? What would be the sound of his voice?

St. John Vianney died in 1859 and was canonized in 1925. His body was found to be incorrupt and was put in a glass casket for veneration.

Chapter 1

The Dialogue of the Saints

(What Led to the Birth of My Letter)

My dear brothers and sisters,

I write from paradise.

Because God is a furnace of love for you, he's asked me to compose a letter and drop it as a postcard from heaven, as if it was my heart. More than that, he has entrusted me with the task of guiding you through these challenging days, when the light of both divine truth and human reason seems to be fading. God desires that you flourish in this moment, even amid the minefield of crises in the family, the Church, and your deeply divided world.

Through the example of my life in Ars, I will show you how.

I am the Curé of Ars, Jean-Marie-Baptiste Vianney, a chosen priest in the line of Melchizedek—an unspectacular and simple man, born in the quiet countryside, where the soil bore the blood of newly martyred French saints. Of all God's priest-saints, I am among the most unlettered, the most unusual, and, by the world's standards, even the most unsightly. To some, I seemed like a cassocked dunce. Even in seminary, I was a misfit—a low-IQ, bottom-of-the-class student, but one with perseverance and abiding love for Jesus. They whispered about my "poor head," and yet they couldn't ignore the clear light in my eyes or the quiet and mysterious peace that surrounded me, so they mostly left me to my own devices.

In Ars, my skin-and-bones parish and town perfectly matched my countenance; it was shabby, undistinguished, and unmemorable. My bishop and brethren saw it as the rightful fit for someone like me—a forgettable man of low expectations and little consequence—to begin as a pastor. No one in Ars really knew what to make of me when I arrived that winter day in 1818. But late one evening, a farmer who had fallen away from the Faith saw a flash of light in my parish church. He sneaked in and saw a gaunt figure quietly weeping before a candle. The following day, word spread to Ars's sixty or so families: "This one is not like the others," he told them. He did not know that I had been begging God that night for the conversion and recovery of Ars's souls.

It is quite a task for a home-schooled seminarian—one who was expelled from seminary three times for poor grades—to offer words of wisdom to a generation 165 years after my death. But just as our Father has, at various times, sent our Queen to visit, instruct, and warn his people, he has sent me to do the same for you. Or, in modern terms, he's called me to *coach* you for this moment. Often, it is the poor, the sickly, and the least among us that God calls to prophesize, to bring light in times of darkness. I am but another piece of God's kindling, meant to fuel the fire he intends to ignite in your technologically fragmented society, and in the scandal-haunted Church to which we both belong.

Although God has asked me to coach and counsel you, I know that many of your bishops, clergy, Catholic intellectuals, and formators do not welcome it. In paradise, St. Philomena has revealed it to me. I smile now, dear reader, imagining you asking, *Who is Philomena?* Allow me to briefly share her story, for it is vital that you understand how the ancient child-martyr became the muse and guiding light of my entire priesthood.

When I was fifteen, the tiny skeleton of Philomena was discovered in a forgotten corner of the Roman Catacomb of Priscilla. I was told that the bones of the decapitated girl lay beside a vial of dried blood and an image of an anchor and a palm—three sacred symbols of her willingness to die for Jesus Christ. In that instant of awareness, something profound happened: Philomena seemed to travel through the mysteries of time and pour into my then-timid soul. A light blinked on, a sacred light that never faded. It was on that day that I resolved to become a priest with the native strength and unblinking courage of Philomena. If ordained, I would try to carry her as an icon into my priesthood. She would be the red martyr, in blood; I, the white, through priestly asceticism. Though I called upon her intercession daily in Ars, she remained a mystery in my time.

My dear little saint is no longer a mystery. The "wonder worker" has made many visitations since her discovery at the turn of the nineteenth century. Her story has become widely known: In brief, it is this: After resisting the sexual advances of the Roman Emperor Diocletian, he subjected her to a series of tortures. She was scourged and dragged through town, then thrown into deep waters with anchors tied around her. After she surfaced minutes later—alive—soldiers were ordered to fasten her to a tree and to shoot arrows into her. Mystifyingly, Philomena survived yet again. Thereafter, Diocletian ordered her head to be removed. The fruits of her brief yet startlingly brave life have echoed far beyond her tomb.

Today, Philomena's name is glorified in heaven. On earth, she was revered throughout the priesthoods of Sts.

Padre Pio, Louis de Montfort, Peter Julian Eymard, and other holy men and women.

In a particular way, my muse brought countless miracles and conversions to Ars through my priesthood. It is she—my tortured friend—who has inspired this letter.

So yes—in paradise, the lioness Philomena revealed to me that many clergy will read my words as little more than a horse-and-buggy pastoral approach—something the Church has "thankfully outgrown" and moved past. A growing number of this modern set have recategorized my care for the welfare of souls as antiquated—or worse, a priestly hazard harmful to their physical and emotional well-being. The tender memories of Ars's revival—its wholesale renewal into a town of willing saints—have mostly been locked away behind presbytery doors. This is disheartening to God, especially since Pope Pius XI, in 1929, declared me to be the model and patron saint of the very priests who regard what unfolded in Ars as pious folklore. But no—behind that locked rectory door is a still-beating heart and the answer that will motivate priests to enter into this time of moral collapse. The sacred secrets of overcoming widespread apathy to the Catholic faith and sparking a revival are buried like thousands of pearls in the soil and story of Ars.

But still, why has God called me—a branch pulled from the fire of seemingly doomed seminary days—to elucidate on ways to bring renewal to the West? I could barely read or even form a proper sentence until I was seventeen.

I will tell you now how this letter came about.

A cosmic event broke my heart—and God's—in 2018 and 2019, when tens of thousands of you, God's faithful, knelt to venerate my incorrupt heart at chapels, shrines, parishes, and basilicas across the United States. Never in the history of your country has so sweeping a dirge risen to paradise as it did then. As the Knights of Columbus reverently carried my heart from state to state, it broke again and again. You came in waves of anguish. Many of you poured out your grief over a single sorrow: you told God—through me—that you had lost your children and loved ones to the world. With blurred eyes and clenched hands, you implored in fierce whispers: *St. John Vianney, go to God. Beg for my children. The world has stolen them. But also find my brothers and sisters, parents, friends, and the hopeless and confused.* In a dimension you cannot see, your pleas—a torrent of sorrow, fear, and loneliness—covered the circumference of heaven.

You begged for your little lambs—your children who'd been lured into the Western world's choking smoke of minimalism, indifference, wokeism, dark ideologies, and the spiritualities of madness. You pleaded and prayed for those close to you, those with whom you share a bond of family, community, work, and yes—even baptism.

God turned to me in paradise then. He stood next to Philomena. The image—God and my patron saint standing side by side—brought tears to my eyes and a lump in my throat. God softly spoke a few words to Philomena, who then turned her gaze to me. God had sent the little martyr to guide me—once again.

It was my muse who spoke the words that prompted this correspondence. *Dear Jean-Marie, they mourn for their lost ones,* she said, staring intently into my glistening eyes. *Beneath this cry, though, is another longing—one for you.*

Philomena . . . I shifted my gaze. *My Lord and my God,* I implored, *explain to this dim soul.*

God looked at me with tenderness, then nodded to Philomena, who continued. *Oh, Curé, they plead for shepherds who will stand firm and fight against Satan's attempts to claim and corrupt souls,* she said. *Deep down, these parents understand that the Bridegroom has always sought out lost lambs. But they cannot find priests with magnanimous hearts like yours, those with a paternal and pastoral impulse to save souls at any cost.*

I stood speechless, my tongue tied.

In the silence, as I took to heart God's commission, my little guide began summoning priests from the heavenly court. Momentarily, Damien the Leper, Pope

Peter, Maximilian Kolbe, John Bosco, Philip Neri, Pio, John Neumann, Francis de Sales, and Patrick stood before us and God. They, too, had been shaken by the plaintive cries before the reliquary of my heart.

The child-martyr leveled her gaze over each of the saints and spoke firmly. *The Father has gathered us to discuss a letter he is asking the holy Curé to write to grieving parents, to those whose children turn away from the sacraments, to those whose friends and family have wandered away from grace. As priest-saints, God has urged that you speak plainly—and with precision—so that together we may strengthen Jean-Marie for the mission entrusted to him by the Father. The Curé must know the stakes of the spiritual war he's been asked to address. His task is to bring the sweet fire of his priesthood in Ars into the open hearts of faithful parents, indeed of all those who love heaven more than they love earth.* God remained silent, allowing Philomena's words to settle deep in the souls of the priest-saints.

After a period of silence, the little lioness explained: *Before we exchange thoughts on the Curé's task, we must discuss what led these faithful disciples to kneel in looming despair before the Curé's heart—and what has led myriads of both young and wearied Catholic souls to leave the Faith.*

The priest-saints squared their shoulders, nodding like infantrymen readying for war. In heaven, each had come to regard Philomena as a gladiator. Each of us stood in silence, deferring to the martyr-pope. Yet Peter, too, remained mute. He knew that Philomena's presence and words would set the stage for what had remained, until now, an unspoken topic in paradise—the piecemeal re-engineering and softening of the ministerial priesthood.

God nodded at the wonder worker, then Philomena spoke once again. *Never in Christendom's history do faithful parents and sincere followers of Christ lament as they do today. Their mournful symphony rises to heaven like the incense of the dead. The Church in the West has failed in her mandate to kill the wolf of Modernism Pope Pius X warned of more than a century ago. Satan has used the gap in the wall to chase legions of children into the thick woods of confusion, where their power to reason is met by the gauntlet of modern educators who lead them astray: relativists, entertainers, Marxists, Luciferians, pagans, and the like. Even the young ones who've managed to escape are awash in a septic current which has flooded their often-unformed souls.*

But it is not only children and adolescents who suffer beneath the weight of the culture. Many adults, too, have lost the power of reason. Countless millions of them do not pray. We do not speak of it in heaven, but the sexual revolution and sexual identity crisis are killing souls. Although the demons steal souls through modern technological devices, many parents give them to their children as unlimited-use toys, which befoul their tender souls in the fashion of Ouija boards.

The martyr paused and a chill filled the space. God's eyes had become fiery orbs. The priest-saints and I looked down at heaven's floor, afraid of his countenance, but Philomena stood erect and sympathetically studied the Father's face. We dared to lift our heads when a rumbling began to shake the heavens, and we beheld paradise bathed in a red light that stretched as far as we could see.

The wisdom in Peter's quiet deference was silently admired by the priest-saints and me. Philomena's plainspokenness established the tone of our dialogue and shaped the words of my letter.

God turned to me and looked at me with tender expectation, before looking to Philomena once more. *Priests*, she exclaimed, *when these parents cry out for their children, when these lonely and discouraged faithful cry out for their families, friends, and neighbors—they cry for Jean-Marie! They want a man willing to give away his life, like a log meant for the fire. Yet too many priests have chosen their own comfort over the fight!* The brave-hearted child paused, her eyes flashing. *As priests, each of you embraced your vocation in the trenches of spiritual war—you understood comfort was a form of corruption, and you fought it off ruthlessly, as if it was Satan himself.*

The priest-titans nodded uniformly as heaven's blaze began to soften, shifting to the violet hue that lights the underside of clouds at the close of day. The priest of joy spoke first. *The great news is that these good-hearted Catholics still believe there are shepherds with self-emptying love. Their words are heartbeats of hope!* offered St. Philip Neri.

Through his Old Testament beard, St. Kolbe spoke with a voice that sounded like a tremor and steered the conversation back to its purpose by quoting Scripture: *When I was a child, I used to talk as a child, think as a child, reason as a child; When I became a man, I put aside childish things. . . . Paul's words have been ignored by many of today's modern bishops and priests. Instead of embracing their victimhood, too many cling to frequent social outings, social media streams, choice wines, evenings at expensive restaurants, and various forms of nonreligious entertainment. Many too frequently bow their heads to technology and take extended vacations—without their clerical clothes and Roman collar—where they reside in luxurious accommodations. On weekdays, too many choose to sleep in rather than nourishing their early-rising, work-a-day flock with an early Mass.*

I watched the priest-saints lower their heads. No one dared speak, fearing the martyr had spoken too plainly. Each feared looking into the face of God. And still, God remained silent.

The Leper broke the silence, severity lay heavy in his eyes. *Fr. Kolbe is not a prophet of doom; his words are precise. It has gone unmentioned in paradise, but few bishops and priests enter into the crucifixion-of-self their priesthood demands. Because of the cost, many will not embrace the kenosis they promised to God at ordination. They once knew their calling was to strip themselves of worldly comforts, but so few do.*

St. Francis de Sales spoke in a measured but direct manner. *It is true. Many rarely offer their flock the opportunity to have their sins absolved. On this point, Jean-Marie is seen by many to have been a maniac whose confessional became his splintered home for four decades. His marathon days of cleansing souls in his confessional wasn't priestly mania, but rather a demonstration of love.*

The holy missionary from Bohemia, John Neumann, spoke hesitantly. *Yes. Because the Curé was a mortified man stripped of comforts, his inner eye was honed to see penitents' hidden or unknown sins, whereby he could work to purge and uproot them. . . . Many priests will not purify themselves by entering this mortified life, or even offer a fast once a week. Accordingly, their comfort blurs their inner eye and blunts their desire to confront—or even notice—the devil's malice.*

And it must be said, the holy Bishop de Sales added, *The root of the crisis is that many modern clergy are not devoted to prayer. Without this intimate union with Christ, they cannot even see the Starved Man of the Cross, nor fully receive the Blood he pours out for them. As the Curé saw in Robespierre's Judas priests, too many of today's priests have genuflected to the world.*

No one spoke. And God remained silent.

With quiet dignity, the Fisherman looked at God, who nodded. The first pope then gazed intently into the faces of his brothers. His eyes blazed. *There are four predominating faults that weaken the modern priesthood,* Simon Peter began.

First, while many holy priests wake each day with a zeal to save souls, too few present themselves before our Savior in the monstrance to daily adore his Precious Face. The weight of their guilt, the silence, and the overwhelming Presence of Jesus bombard their conscience—so they stay away. Second, many do not meet Our Mother in the Rosary, nor do they place themselves beneath her mantle, leaving their priesthoods maternally unprotected. She is their Queen, but they do not seem to care. Third, because so many priests fail to properly prepare their souls for the Holy Sacrifice of the Mass, they do not pray it with devotion or recognize their role as God's intercessors at the altar, their calling to stand between heaven and earth. For many, the Mass has become a duty rather than a sacred pearl. And finally, because many priests fear the response of their flock and the world, they do not preach on the hard topics of modernity. Their suffocation of the prophetic voice has spiritually contracepted their entire priesthood.

After Simon Peter's diagnosis, no one knew what to say.

The Leper restarted the conversation. *The Pope has uniquely identified the diseased root of the crisis,* he said. *These priests*—he cried out, his voice rising—*they've forgotten who they are!* His voice softened some as he continued. *The parents and penitents who knelt before Vianney's heart are good. Most of them try, day by day, to do their best for their children; they are diligent and mostly solicitous. But let's speak plainly about the millions of other Catholics who share the mindset of the world. They see acts of veneration, the pleas before relics, as nothing more than pious superstition. Many parents have lost their children to the world only after they were lost to the world themselves—and they scarcely consider it. That their children have strayed from the sacraments doesn't even trouble them. And yet, they presume that they will be reunited with their children in heaven. Others straddle the world's fence. Afraid to offend, they fail to inspire, to warn, to help others find the path of salvation. They, too, presume that all will be saved.*

A sudden gust of wind swept through paradise, and a low rumble echoed. No one spoke, but I sensed that the Leper's words—assured salvation—caused the priest-saints to reflect on the countless millions of souls who once shared the same thought, only to find themselves in hell.

Peter spoke above the winds, his voice heavy with sorrow. *The grieving parents who collapsed at the Curé's heart feel abandoned . . . as I, too, abandoned our dear Lord at the Cross. All those who truly believe feel alone.* Peter looked at God, his words laden with sorrow, but the Father remained silent.

Padre Pio spoke, his voice barely a whisper, yet it cut through the driving wind. *The martyr-pope is right about the abandonment,* the stigmatic said. *But we must go deeper. The lost began to stray when they were very young—when they were still witnesses to the Holy Sacrifice. The child, even then, grasped something profound. He saw the inner priest at the altar and knew him. He could sense the light in the priest's eyes, the reverence in his rubrics, the brawn of his prophetic voice, the radiance that shone from within. And when the priest raised Christ's Flesh and Blood, the child instinctively understood the priest's essence by how he held the Slaughtered Lamb in his fingertips. It was then that the child unconsciously understood whether or not the priest cared for his soul.*

God gazed into the eyes of his persecuted stigmatic; his expression filled with tender affection. *Yes, Pio*, St. Philip said in a low tone. *You were one who vanished into your identity for as many as three hours to offer the Sacrifice; you understood the deeper reality and the harm caused by a poorly celebrated Mass. The wandering child was not always lost. Children raised by spiritual fathers—by priests who appeared to the marveling child as having crawled into the skin of the Son at the Consecration—are the remnant-children. These children have been given a great and difficult challenge. Their plight is heralding Christ and his living truth to a generation that will largely reject and even hate them.*

And that is why, the Leper said, politely breaking in, *even the remnant often goes underground, refusing their impulse to share their love of Christ and his Good News. The devil has suffocated the voice of God by strangling believers with fear of the world. The West's cluster of modern heresies has caused countless believers to bury Truth beneath the bushel basket of private devotion and thought.*

St. Patrick spoke gravely as the wind began to settle. *The silence of believers today is the inverse of the Great Commission,* he said in a whisper. *Snakes are coiled now in every shadow, hidden in every corner of the West and beyond. We see how the serpents have returned—they are everywhere on my island. And yet . . . few will work to drive them out.*

Peter met Patrick's gaze, his eyes heavy and mournful. He remembered the thousands upon thousands of Celts and Druids that Patrick had baptized, after patiently explaining the mystery of the Triune God through the shamrock. *Oh, Patrick, how heaven laments the return of the*

Great Hunger to your land, the pestilence of secularism that grips Irish souls. Though there remains a faithful remnant clinging to the ancient faith, they often retreat from the truth that lives in them. These quiet believers are not alone; they are like the millions of other Catholics across the globe—living in the shadows, uncertain how to confront the world with the Gospel. Too many fear rejection, terrified of being branded as true followers of Jesus Christ. They dread being cast off as interlopers for standing firm in the Gospel and speaking against the venomous lies of modernity.

The Leper spoke then, his voice as weary as the centuries themselves. *Yes, it is a famine of courage. Ireland's quiet believers—all those who fear the judgment of the world—weigh the world's opinion before considering the destiny of their eternal souls. The world seems devoid of heroes, of those willing to sacrifice all, to die as Christ did.*

The saints fell silent, each lost in thought over the vanishing heroes in their native lands, and how the gaping hole had given birth to spreading godlessness. For a long, somber time, no one spoke. In the silence, I did my best to recall the glories of Ars at the end of my life, and of the hardy souls of converted French men and women in the spiritually resurrected nation. But then I winced when an image came of what had become of the "Eldest Daughter of the Church." I saw my entire country, like Notre Dame Cathedral, engulfed in an inferno. Then, a more gruesome image emerged: France had become Joan of Arc, writhing, in full flame.

I scanned the faces of the priest-saints. They, too, had become lost in a sorrowful reverie over modern apathy to heroism, over those from their native land who had rejected the moral strength to fight Satan.

Thankfully, the merry pied piper of children, ever eager to shift the mood, seized the silence and threw his hands into the air with enthusiasm, gesturing as if urging a waiter to rush fresh pasta to a table. Smiling widely, St. Bosco bellowed, *Damien loved his family of lepers so much, he became one with them! When the Leper docked his boat, he amputated every shred of comfort and consolation to save the abandoned ones.* His voice lowered some as he continued, *The Leper—each of us here—surrendered our lives to God. And then, in various forms of martyrdom, we began to die. This is what true heroes do.*

That, my dear Bosco, is the heart of it, Philomena exclaimed, her voice rising like a lioness protecting her pride. *Many parents will not become like God's Son—the Victim who poured himself out with no consolations. The Leper fought leprosy by nailing himself to the cross of the lepers he loved. Today's dads and moms must fight this same way. But they must fight something deadlier than leprosy—they must fight for children against the surging tide of modern evil. Only the love of the martyrs suffices today. As the Leper died for his flock, so too must these parents, these family members, these friends and neighbors. It is their burden! Their lost children and loved ones are the world's victims; they must become Christlike victims to save them!*

It was time, God knew, to end the dialogue. He had been carefully observing me listening to the back-and-forth.

The Curé's letter will be addressed to parents, Philomena said, imparting God's command. *The Father has asked him to share the memories of his holy life and to recount the stories that helped shepherd Ars back to grace. The Curé is a prophet for these times because the qualities of shepherding are immutable. His memories will serve these parents well and provide a spiritual blueprint to map out ways to keep their children in the fold. His story will refresh the compassion these believers have for their families, friends, and neighbors. Curé, there was never a day when you didn't die to yourself to save. Write of this way. Write to them the story of Ars.*

When she finished speaking, Philomena looked lovingly into the Father's face. God smiled at her with the warmth of thousands of sunsets. Then, for the first time since the dialogue began, she left the Father's side.

Philomena began to walk toward me. She was smiling—smiling widely, like a small child on a snowy Christmas morning. She carried something in her hand. *Oh*, I yelped interiorly. It was my old writing quill from Ars, the one I had used to write so many letters to my family, the trusty pen with which I had scratched out hundreds of sermons. Her gift rendered me wordless. In the silence, Philomena wrapped her arms around me, burying her head in my chest, like a daughter embracing her father before he leaves for war. Heaven became bathed in gold. After some time, she lifted her heels off the ground and whispered into my ear: *You were my muse, too.* The priest-saints quietly regarded us, their eyes glistening.

With her parting words, she stepped away and back to the side of the Father. There she raised her hands in prayer. *Jean-Marie—it is a time like never before, when all faithful Catholics must look to themselves and their own common priesthood. They cry for you to help them rise to meet the challenge. You must guide them now.* The saints lowered their heads, murmuring prayers of supplication.

It is time to bestow on you a second name; you are no longer only the patron saint of parish priests. In this time of clergy crisis, God gives you a new name: Jean-Marie, from this moment and forevermore, you are the Patron of the Domestic Priesthood.

I looked, bewildered, into Philomena's eyes. But I saw a quiet confidence, as if she knew something I didn't. The priest-saints had fallen to their knees, heads bowed. Then I looked into the face of God, whose assuring nod, I knew, had given birth to the name he had known from the beginning of time. When I saw that his eyes were filled with fatherly pride, my soul took flight. *Write from your heart, dear Jean-Marie,* Philomena continued, as she and the Father began to walk, side by side, back to his throne, to Jesus and his Mother. The priest-saints took to their feet again as Philomena offered a final plea on behalf of God. *These restless Catholics prayed at your indomitable heart. Now—give your heart back to them.*

The priest-saints watched the Father and his spiritual daughter walk hand in hand back to the throne of adoration.

Finally, Simon Peter spoke a last word, his voice heavy with solemnity. *A final thought, holy Curé: Though they may not say it, these millions of wandering children long for the firm and loving discipline of a father and the deep maternal embrace of a mother. All men and women are called to love in this way. Deep down, these lost sheep hunger for Jesus, and they will encounter him through parents—and others—who pour themselves out as he did. You must show these Catholics how to die each day.*

The crucified pope continued: *All of us must make the ultimate sacrifice. Parents must trade their own life for the life of their child. Family members, friends, and neighbors must sacrifice and willingly lay down their lives to help bring the lost ones back. Many millions of souls are at stake.*

With those words, the priest-saints stood in silent reverence. *We'll leave you now to write,* Peter added quietly with a wide grin, his ruddy face full of trust. *Praise God for this work to be accomplished through you.*

As the priest-saints turned toward the throngs of angels and saints gathered before the throne, the merry one cried out, his voice ringing with a joyful, almost childlike exuberance—like a Christmas wassail pouring from his soul: *The Curé*, St. Philip Neri heralded like a Bethlehem angel. *Brothers—the Curé* is *the cure!*

Each priest-saint smiled and, one by one, walked away. Abruptly, I was left alone—until a second gale-force wind swept through the air. Then came a piercing light, and I knew it was the angelic warrior, Michael. As the thunderous beat of his wings faded, he stood before me like a bright Alleluia of hope for the world.

Mary has sent me to you, he said, his deep voice filled with serene urgency. *She's sent me to you with a personal request—and perhaps an insight.*

The great archangel looked directly into my eyes, his face resolute. Despite the weariness from the untold wars he had fought down the millennia, he stood before me as powerful as I had ever seen him, a gladiator radiating solidity and resolve. *Curé, you are one like me,* he said, his voice carrying the weight of shared struggle. *You, too, fought Satan relentlessly. Mary's request is this: Beg parents to use every weapon at their disposal to protect their children. Proclaim this to them on her behalf: "Disciples—wield the fullness of your faith for the salvation of fallen souls." Every day, the Queen of heaven sees what I do: the beast is growing, expanding. I am fighting an evil today that I have never seen, nor could have ever imagined.*

With a tone like thunder, Michael's next words pierced through the stillness: *Curé, tell them this: I need them to fight to the death to save their children, their families, their friends, and yes, their fading shepherds and parishes.*

I need their help.

The warrior-angel gripped my shoulder, his hand strong and firm. His gaze lingered, as if binding our hearts in a shared mission. For a moment, time seemed to stop.

I will do my best for Mary and you. My words were insufficient and meager, but they were all I could muster.

When Michael shifted his enormous wings and turned to leave, I suddenly found words tumbling from my mouth: *Please, Michael, before you take flight, tell me —what is Mary's insight?*

*Ah, yes—*of *course! It is this, John. As you have come to understand, God has given you your task at this hour because of your holy priesthood. But he has chosen you for a second reason.* Michael was smiling widely. *It is because you chose Philomena.*

I looked at the mighty angel, perplexed.

He spoke to my confusion: *Satan is waging his greatest assaults today against priesthoods in churches and homes—*

but just as lethal, just as violent, is his war to steal the purity from God's young ones. Michael's eyes narrowed, his brow furrowed. *He pours his venom into the pure souls of youth everywhere.*

But Curé—there will be a mighty wind at your back as you work to bring priests back into homes; Philomena will be standing next to you. When you chose her as a child, she became something mightier than a muse. She became like me—she became a guardian angel who never left your side. The same holds true now and forevermore.

As you begin God's task, Philomena will be the unspoken witness to purity, chaste living, and the endless fight in which parents must engage to guard the souls in their care.

Michael let his words penetrate.

Then, without warning, he embraced me fiercely, and with a final, resounding beat of his wings, he began his descent back down to the dark places of the earth.

Dear reader, I am left alone with my quill.

So I begin:

I am Jean-Marie-Baptiste Vianney, a priest ordained by the skin of his teeth. I was once rejected, the poor one; lonesome, ill-regarded—the seminary failure. And I am the one God has chosen at this hour to write.

But isn't this just his way?

St. John Vianney spent countless hours in this confessional, a place of charity and mercy for tens of thousands of sinners.

Chapter 2

Portraits of Humility

(The Virtue that Helps the World Flourish)

To begin my letter, I'd like to start at the end. I want you to see Ars after its lost years, after my flock had shifted from apathy and decadence to a land reborn, where order and grace took root. I am no artist, but I will do my best to paint a few images of my little farming community as it underwent its mid-nineteenth-century moral transformation. I once said: "Sometimes the mere sight of a picture is enough to move and convert us; at times, pictures make almost as deep an impression as the objects they represent."[2]

2. Richard Conlin, "Summary of The Curé d'Ars by Abbé Francis Trochu," *The Prodigal Catholic*, August 14, 2018, https://prodigalcatholic.com/2018/08/14/summary-of-the-cure-dars-by-abbe-francis-trochu-2/.

But before I begin to paint, dear reader, it is necessary for you to look at the degenerate images of Ars's bygone days, and the cabinet of mineral spirits I used to rub out the lust, drunkenness, greed, gossip, sloth, and spiritual bankruptcy. Picture, if you will, the village as it once was—a place where sin and neglect had dulled the hearts of its people, where the parish church was empty, taverns and cabarets full, and the streets quiet with indifference. Do you see, dear reader, the old Ars in your fallen world as it is today? The mortal sin in Ars couldn't be uprooted and ended through private prayer and effort alone.

My village required a saint, so from my earliest days as an uncertain curé, I explored the saints' holy manner. I began to read each night from *The Lives of the Saints,* and that is how I absorbed the wisdom of the souls of those who saved broken families, marriages, towns, and even nations. The tales of these paragons gave me libraries of sacred secrets, but it seemed to me that two characteristics—humility and the fire of their charity—emerged like three-dimensional images rising off every page. So, it would be through humble acts and love that I would begin to try to turn Ars inside out.

For now, I will fast-forward through the grueling years that led to Ars's eventual resurrection—which the following chapters unpack—to show how my hard-bitten flock became meek and more kindly; the very reflection of virtues I strove to pour out on them. Because I knew that grace and transformation often found its first heartbeat through acts of humility, I worked to examine each of my defects and hints of my own pride and strove to annihilate them. Thereafter, I resolved, with God's grace, to respond to every cruelty with meekness, even when it deeply hurt me to do so. Often, being considered a fool came at a cost. But because this was the fashion in which Jesus commanded me to shepherd, I absorbed calumnies, ostracization, and mockery over and over again and—without ducking—turned the other cheek.

I encourage you now to use your Catholic imagination and envision the images I will now paint of piety in my village; hang them as portraits onto the walls of your soul. I want you to truly *see* how broken families healed and children, teenagers, and young adults—oh, those amorous young adults—returned to catechism classes and the sacraments with zeal and joy, not fear. In time, you may come to see that these images are not merely representations of a past moment, but living icons that can be painted onto today—interior invitations that call you to the same renewal of spirit that transformed Ars. I beg you, friends, to see how the virtue of humility can steer the lost lambs in your own life back to the Savior.

I first came to truly understand the power of humility during my seemingly doomed seminary days, as I became painfully aware of my many weaknesses and limitations. My dearest friend and savior of my vocation, Fr. Charles Balley, stayed full of cheer as he continuously worked to steer me past my classroom struggles. After a number of failing exams, my mentor told me that the virtue of humility, which Thomas Aquinas called the queen of virtues, would be the sturdiest piece of driftwood I could cling to in my upstream swim to become a priest. But the holy Fr. Balley didn't need to speak of Aquinas; it was through his own action that I saw the virtue up close. His patience with me was heroic as he lavished me with his time, good humor, and wisdom each day to guide me over my hurdles.

But I didn't know the cost and demand of humility until the day, as a twenty-eight-year-old seminarian, I was slapped hard across the face by a minor seminarian who was nearly half my age. The cassocked teenager had grown exasperated by the stammering of my poorly remembered Latin conjugations. At the sting of the slap, my thoughts turned to Christ's command, "If any one strikes you on the right cheek, turn to him the other also" (Mt 5:39), so I knelt at the feet of my young tutor and asked his forgiveness for causing his wrath. Thereafter, the young man broke down and begged for mercy. Do you see, dear reader, the cost of humility? More importantly—do you see its power to convert? To further clarify, I will paint more images.

Years later as a priest, after a meeting of minds of influential clergy in and around Lyons, a formal complaint was to be sent to the bishop of Belley seeking my removal as pastor of Ars. Examples of my harsh proclamations on hell from the pulpit, mischievousness, theological dimwittedness, and my wild-eyed approaches to saving souls were cited in the letter that called me a danger to my people. When an abashed friend showed me the petition, I took the letter that condemned my priesthood, read it with swollen eyes, and signed my name. Tears immediately sprang to my friend's eyes as he walked away to spread the news of what he called an astonishing endorsement of their sentiments. God, of course, handled the fallout; the few priests and handful of townsfolk who signed the petition began to regard me differently, and pleaded for my forgiveness. I imagine it was because I agreed with their thoughts on my insufficiency that I survived as the curé of Ars.

Once, a man of some prominence and education entered the sacristy and said, "Monsieur le Curé, I am not coming to confession. I have come to reason with you." I responded, "Oh! My good friend, you are making a great mistake," I said. "I do not know how to reason."[3] In time, the skeptic became a faithful Catholic.

Years later, on May 3, 1845, curiosity brought the intellectual giant and preacher Fr. Jean-Baptiste Henri-Dominique Lacordaire to Ars. The French Dominican, who was considered by many to be the world's greatest public orator, entered my church at around five o'clock in the morning, where I had been hearing confessions since two hours prior. He introduced himself before Mass and briefly shared that word had spread on his travels about the work of the lowly pastor who holds this pen. *Praise God*, I thought at the time. *Aquinas meets the dumb ox.*

At Mass, I preached on the Holy Spirit and expounded on the Advocate as the "gardener of our souls."[4] I imagine it was the same Spirit that moved Fr. Lacordaire to rush up to me following Mass to exclaim: "You taught me to know the Holy Spirit!"[5] Thereafter, we became fast friends. For two days we discussed the good God on long walks in the countryside. We prayed the Office together. He instructed my community in catechism and sang Vespers with them.

3. Michel de Saint Pierre, *The Remarkable Curé of Ars: The Life and Achievements of St. John Mary Vianney*, trans. M. Angeline Bouchard (Doubleday, 1963), p. 147.

4. "Father Lacordaire, OP," Extract from the Annales d'Ars (May–June 2009), Parish and Shrine of Ars, https://www.arsnet.org/en/ars-great-witnesses/father-lacordaire-op/.

5. "Father Lacordaire, OP."

Before parting ways, the famous preacher fell to his knees to ask for my blessing.

A few days later, a priest friend of Fr. Lacordaire, who learned he had visited Ars, asked about the purported inelegance of my preaching style. The Dominican responded: "[The curé] preached as a good curé should preach," he said, noting my humility. "That holy priest has uttered, in a striking manner, a thought in connection with the Holy Ghost which I myself have been pondering for a very long time."[6] I later told a friend who asked about the unlikely visit from the great preacher of Notre-Dame de Paris, "You know the saying 'extremes meet'; well, it was realized yesterday in the pulpit of Ars, where extreme knowledge and extreme ignorance were seen."[7]

As the transformation of Ars became known throughout much of Europe, photographers were sent to my village to capture an image of the man they were told was the "holy curé" who had raised Ars from its slumber. Although I told the men with cameras they were grossly misled and implored them to return home without my photograph, they persisted. So, frequently I was forced to run down the streets of town screaming and acting like the resident court jester of Ars. When they regarded

6. Abbé François Trochu, *The Cure D'Ars: St. Jean-Marie-Baptiste Vianney* (TAN Books, 1977), p. 489.

7. Trochu, p. 490.

me as an imbecile, they left town, dejected. They had been misinformed; Ars's pastor, they now saw, had lost his mind.

As I decreased, Ars seemed to increase. Competitive farmers, who once regarded their neighbors with suspicion, began to meet at fence lines to exchange long-hidden secrets of husbandry and agriculture. They mended fallen fence posts without a word, or chased off potato-eating gophers, crows, and deer—quiet acts of kindness for a neighbor done in the hope they wouldn't be noticed. Families struggling to make ends meet and snakebitten farmers often awoke to find pies, stews, sacks of seeds, notes of encouragement, and envelopes heavy with francs left on their porches. Hardened men, once distant and rough, began holding their beaming wives' hands as they walked together through town and into Sunday Mass.

I cannot express how deeply satisfying it was to see these slow-moving waves of benevolence spreading across Ars. By God's grace, and through a constant effort of prayer and pastoral care, something miraculous began to happen. One by one, the hearts of my people were awakened to the virtues of humility and charity. I was watching a town flower into a humble kingdom in which people desired little more than to offer themselves as gifts to their neighbors. The pews filled, not just with bodies, but with souls eager to become saints. The confessional lines grew longer as the people came, not out of obligation but out of a profound desire to finally shed their old ways and become holy.

Dear reader, I paint these examples to show how the virtue of humility serves as a winepress for you. When you take this narrow path—even when your innermost self screams for you to take a more exalted way—you will begin to be crushed into a libation that pours into the deepest recesses of your fallen-away loved ones. But I must warn you: Because the Evil One knows how this queen of virtues manages to conquer and melt the most hardened hearts and minds, he will continually spin lie after lie about your own entitlements, self-worth, and dignity. This was how Satan immobilized and corrupted Adam and Eve, and how he's damned countless souls since. Beneath hell's seventh ring lays the bedrock that carries the weight of Satan's entire kingdom: It is the deadly sin of Pride.

Ah, but I am one of the fortunate ones. God did me the great favor of endowing me with no gifts or talents. As a young priest, I felt there were only deficiencies, fears, and poor sins in me. But even then, the volume of my shortcomings and sins was unknown. But the more I chose the path of humility, the more I came to know my weaknesses. My humiliations were reason for celebration, because they enabled me to fall even more into the ocean of God's mercy as I begged for his wisdom and aid.

If you've read the previous few pages of my letter, it means I've managed to sink the hook. I wanted to take you to the period of time I spent with Fr. Antoine Raymond, when my resolve to stay in the grace of humility and charity was tested for many years. It was poor Fr. Raymond who offered me an opportunity to pour myself out in humility, as Christ did when he bled out on the Cross.

I will never forget the autumn day in 1845 when Fr. Raymond arrived in Ars to become my parochial vicar. The bishop told the young priest that my years of sleeping on cold floors and my winter days of hearing confessions had given me pleuropneumonia and facial neuralgia. He asked Fr. Raymond to assist me in whatever capacity I thought was necessary.

I felt singularly blessed. I had known of Fr. Raymond when he was in seminary. When I had been told he was a serious-minded and diligent young man who lacked the financial resources to pay for his tuition, I covered his expenses and purchased his first cassock without his knowledge.

When he arrived, I saw that he carried the bearing of a priest with great ambition and confidence. After welcoming him into the presbytery, he asked to be directed to his sleeping quarters. I told him of the predicament: There was just one bedroom. Soon thereafter, he began to unpack in that bedroom, the same one I had used for the previous two decades. Perhaps sensing my declining health would soon end my pastorship in Ars—or even my life—Fr. Raymond arrived with the ambition to become the new curé of Ars.

When a few townsfolk heard about Fr. Raymond's selection of bedrooms, they reached for their pitchforks. Thereafter, understanding his rashness, the determined priest was given lodging in town. My friend, Mademoiselle Catherine Lassagne, said to me then that Fr. Raymond was "sent by God to try the patience of his faithful servant, who looked upon himself as a guardian rather than an auxiliary."[8] Although parishioners viewed Fr. Raymond's manner as brusque and egocentric and as one who belabored over what he believed to be clever or pious thoughts in his sermons, I appreciated his wisdom and charisma. When my parishioners complained about what they believed was an overweening confidence from the pulpit, I defended the young priest and told them his manner was just a mirror of his confidence in the Lord.

8. Trochu, p. 504.

"I don't know if it's because I love him," I said at the time, "but I think he preaches well."[9]

As the years moved on, Fr. Raymond began to rebuke me for what he deemed were imprudent pastoral decisions. He questioned the habits of my penances and began to publicly criticize my behavior in his sermons. A growing number of villagers became incensed over a man they saw as unholy and absurd. But I loved Fr. Raymond with even greater tenderness then, understanding that the man, twenty years my junior, simply needed time to mature. While my parishioners confessed that they couldn't comprehend what they saw as the heroic patience and charity I showed toward him, they acknowledged that the example of my humility had inspired them to strive for the same virtue. They observed how my love for the young priest deepened, even as his flaws, harshness, and arrogance became more pronounced. Thankfully, my flock understood that I was not just their shepherd, but Fr. Raymond's as well. They recognized my care for him, despite the many challenges he posed, and came to appreciate the patience and commitment I showed, knowing it was all for his spiritual growth. I said to them at that time, "Humility is to the various virtues what the

9. "Father Antoine Raymond," Extract from the Annales d'Ars (November–December 2010), Parish and Shrine of Ars, https://www.arsnet.org/en/ars-great-witnesses/father-antoine-raymond/.

chain is in a rosary: Take away the chain and the beads are scattered; remove humility, and all the virtues vanish."[10]

When a delegate from the chancery was sent to investigate what he had been told was Fr. Raymond's untoward behavior, I told him:

> Let me keep him; he is not afraid to tell me the truth about myself. How grateful I am to him. . . . I have nothing special to tell your Lordship concerning M. Raymond, except that he deserves a warm place in your heart in return for all his goodness to me. Never give credence to those wicked tongues that are everlastingly retailing evil.[11]

One day in Holy Week, I read a letter detailing Fr. Raymond's indiscretions and pomposity. When I heard it was to be mailed that day to the bishop, I tore it into pieces. My thought was that "Our Lord carried his Cross during these sacred days; surely I can do as he did."[12]

In time, Fr. Raymond began to see with greater vision. When he came to terms with the fact that the thousands of souls traveling to Ars were not seeking him for counsel, absolution, and direction, he requested a transfer and got it in 1853. Thereafter, as he began to pastor his new flock at a small parish in Polliat, he began to slowly transform

10. Conlin.
11. Trochu, p. 506.
12. Trochu, p. 507.

into a humble countryside pastor, conformed to grace by the humiliation of his pride.

Much later, when Fr. Raymond heard I was in the throes of dying, he left his parish and raced to my bedside. In tears, he kissed me. He explained in tender words that my unfailing measures of patience and charity for him had seeped into his soul—and saved it.

In the wake of my passing, the words from a sermon I gave many years earlier were remembered:

> My children, we are, in reality, only what we are in the eyes of God, and nothing more. Is it not quite clear and evident that we are nothing, that we can do nothing, that we are very miserable? Can we lose sight of our sins, and cease to humble ourselves? If we were to consider well what we are, humility would be easy to us, and the demon of pride would no longer have any room in our heart.[13]

A Thought on Humility

I once said to my parishioners: "Do not try to please everybody. Try to please God, the angels, and the saints—they are your public."[14] *Humility is the fastest and surest way to peace*

13. St. John Vianney, "St. John Vianney on Pride," *Catholicism Pure & Simple*, March 21, 2012, https://catholicismpure.wordpress.com/2012/03/21/st-john-vianney-on-pride/.

14. Kathryn Jean Lopez, "St. John Vianney's Relic Reminds Us True Holiness Is Possible for All," *Angelus News,* February 14, 2019, https://angelusnews.com/voices/st-john-vianneys-relic-reminds-us-true-holiness-is-possible-for-all/.

because this queen of virtues removes any consideration of the world's esteem. A tried-and-true solution to expelling the pride of the world from your soul is walking the path of humility.

- Meditate upon Christ's words in Luke 14:7–14.
- Are you a soul who struggles with pleasing God alone? Why do you think this is difficult for you? What are ways in which you can remove concern for pleasing anyone other than God alone? Perhaps consider reading the lives of the saints.
- Do you struggle with the deadly sin of pride? If so, how will you begin the work of eliminating your sense of self-importance and superiority? Perhaps begin by placing yourself in the presence of God and meditating on his knowledge of your sins.
- Ask Jesus, who chose to come as a humble, helpless infant and who "humbled himself and became obedient unto death, even death on a cross" (Phil 2:8), to deliver you from the fear of being forgotten, ridiculed, or wronged, and from the desire of being esteemed, honored, and approved, but instead to help you find comfort and peace in littleness.

St. John Vianney ate small meals out of penance. It was in this humble kitchen that he prepared his small meals, which mostly consisted of potatoes.

Chapter 3

Praying Through the Mist

(The Primacy of Prayer)

Now, dear reader, let us go back to the start.

What biographers have written about what I promised the shepherd boy on that cold winter day in the La Dombes valley is true. The countryside had been bombarded with low-lying clouds, and I had lost the path to Ars. Thanks be to God, I saw the shadowy image of a lad, whose name I discovered was Antoine Givre. He was with a few of his companions in the distance tending their flock. I asked Antoine, the first soul of Ars to greet me as *Curé,* to point me in the right direction. As he worked to reorient me, I felt my soul overcome with joy and found myself wanting to guide and direct *him*. I looked the boy in the eye and thrust my finger high into the mist. "You have shown me the way to Ars," I said, then found myself suddenly announcing to the shepherd, as if I had become a Bethlehem angel, "I shall show you the way to heaven."[15] But instead of walking little Antoine down to a stable with a newborn King, I was taking him, in a supernatural dimension, to his eternal reward. Few know this fact, but I will share it here: My promise to Antoine became a prophecy. When I died many years later, my little wayfinder was the first to follow me.[16]

As I continued traveling the path, I saw an image like a black-and-white postcard of poverty emerge in the valley, where a scattering of thatched cottages, small farm homes, and nondescript huts were boxed in by endless acres of farmland. I made out the poor church in the gloom. It sat forlorn and unimpressive, seemingly the runt of the litter of France's glistening throng of majestic cathedrals, shrines, and ornately stained-glass village parishes. I thought then: *Ha! My parish resembles me.* As I stood in wonder, my spirit divined the future and I could not help whooping into the valley below, as if I had slipped into the skin of all three of Alexandre Dumas's idealistic musketeers. "How small it all is. Yet this parish

15. Trochu, p. 113.
16. Trochu, p. 113.

will not be able to contain the multitude of those who shall journey here."[17] These years later, I see that my first two declarations outside of Ars became fulfilled in a dimension I could never have imagined.

Soon after hurrying down the incline, invigorated by the task before me, I began to feel my bulletproof vest of innocence, fervor, and guilelessness peel away from my body and drop to the ground. Honestly, I never thought about reaching for it again. For the first time in my life, I absorbed the aftershock of a brokenhearted people carrying the unseen shrapnel of war, fatherlessness, and sacramental famine.

As I began to walk through Ars, souls passed me by with not so much as a nod. A few returned hellos with whispered *bonjours*, their faces downturned. Other than the tinkle of cowbells, Ars was noiseless. As I walked on, the unmistakable scent of stale beer and wine hung heavy in the air, betraying the events of the previous night. Without knowing, I walked past three small taverns. I began to sense that Ars had been trapped in a long winter. From paradise, I now know a few of its previous pastors were "juror priests"—that is, they were clergy members who had shorn their configuration to Christ by signing the oath of loyalty to Robespierre's revolutionary

17. George William Rutler, *St. John Vianney: The Curé d'Ars Today* (Ignatius Press, 1988), p. 97.

government. Although a number of previous pastors in Ars were faithful and good, too many were not. I couldn't have known it that day, but the betrayal from Ars's Judas priests had left the town spiritually adrift and caught in the habits of repeated sin. All but a handful of the village's 280-some residents had strayed from the sacraments. The village had little love for God.

With a tarpaulin of grief suddenly covering me, I decided to wander out into the countryside, where I hoped the company of hearty men and farmers would bring some relief. But I quickly sensed that I was mostly just an intrusion, and that the men of Ars kept to their fields on Sundays. *Goodness*, I thought. *I'm going to have a devil of a time convincing them to trade their scythe and pitchfork for a missal and a coin for the poor . . . Oh dear God, these hardworking men believe tending their land is worthier than receiving Your Flesh.* Millet's charming portrait of *The Angelus* would be painted some forty years later; the very inverse of the image I saw that day.

As I left the fields and quickened my footsteps toward St. Sixtus, a dark question rushed over me: *When the church bells pealed on Sunday, would I be preaching to empty pews?* As a sudden lonesomeness came over me, I knew the war Fr. Balley had warned of had begun. I just didn't expect the Evil One to emerge so quickly. But this marked the first day Grappin (as I nicknamed the devil) and I began our decades-long war—and I hadn't even set foot in the shelter of my church to beg for God's aid.

At St. Sixtus, I opened a door and saw before me what seemed a plain and inelegant sanctuary. A small rack of unlit votive candles was set off to each side of the humble nave. Other than the dim light of the sanctuary lamp, not a single candle flickered. In the shadows, I was able to see that Christ's altar was tiny and unadorned, like a newborn baby rejected by his mother. There was no statuary, no adoring angels on either side of the small tabernacle, not even portraits of saints. Thin stained-glass windows cast flat light. Paint was peeling from a few walls; fissures ran down a few others. I fell at the altar and wept. It was the happiest moment of my life.

Biographer Abbé François Trochu rightfully wrote of the "instinct of conquest"[18] I carried with me in those early days. He couldn't have known, though, how the instinct was a weapon of war that opened in me then. I didn't want to convert the world; I just wanted the few hundred souls of Ars. Already, I sensed Grappin would do all in his power to maintain the status quo. I knew right then the Evil One was already at work to become my Siamese twin.

18. Trochu, p. 125.

Prayer that day seemed as important as my next breath, but it also served as my blueprint. Whatever the Holy Spirit revealed to me about the reasons for Ars's faithlessness, I knew, would act as a torchlight, my greatest spiritual weapon to fight Satan for souls. Trochu seemed to crawl into my soul when he wrote of my instinct that day that I had resolved:

> to bring back the indifferent; to convert open and public evil-doers; above all, to persevere in prayer to God from whom all blessings flow; to sanctify himself so as to be able to sanctify others, to offer expiation for the sins of those who refused to do penance for themselves. How weak and helpless he felt when he considered the magnitude of his task! But his soul was filled with a divine energy and God makes choice of the helplessness of the lonely ones to crush the power of human pride.[19]

I remained at my parish throughout the night and pleaded with God to have pity on me and my poor flock. As has been accurately recorded, I implored that night,

> "My God, grant me the conversion of my parish; I am willing to suffer all my life whatsoever it may please Thee to lay upon me; yes, even for one hundred years am I prepared to endure the sharpest pains, only let my people be converted."[20]

19. Trochu, p. 121.
20. Trochu, p. 125.

Even on that first day, I had absorbed Ars into my heart.

That first night I became a beggar-priest in front of the tabernacle. In the days and weeks that followed, if there was a sick call, a passerby or pilgrim seeking absolution, a poor man in need of a meal, or any other pastoral need, townsfolk directed folks to the front pew at St. Sixtus. The kneeler in front of the tabernacle became like my hermit's cell, a place where I rested my head against Jesus's bosom and awaited a word or two in response to my only question: *Loving God, how do I save these souls?* As I awaited his voice, I prayed from my breviary, the trusty lifeline I called my "faithful companion." Usually after Compline, I found myself routinely being pulled to contemplative prayer, where images of a wearied Christ emerged. He appeared forlorn and bloodied on the Cross, wordless—as if he was looking at me through tear-stained eyes and pleading: *John, you will save these souls when you become their victim.* I had my answer.

Loving Savior—I will try! I gasped. *Just give me the strength and wisdom to know how!*

Thereafter, my prayers seemed to have thrust a dual-edged sword into me. One side cut away my feelings of powerlessness and incompetence; the other served as a killing instrument to sever Grappin's grip on Ars. I couldn't have known then that I would drive this sword into Satan's gut the next four decades, as he fought me relentlessly from stealing the tens of thousands of souls who came to my confessional.

Although my priesthood was in its infancy, I knew Ars could eventually be opened to receiving God's grace if I devoted myself to them in prayer. I knew what God told Jeremiah: "Call to me and I will answer you, and will tell you great and hidden things which you have not known" (Jer 33:3). As Ars kept to its self-instituted sacramental moratorium, my spirit sagged. I sometimes grew weary in prayer.

On those nights, though, I always managed to revive myself through the memories of my past, which became for me a sacred amphitheater of splendorous images of my hometown Dardilly at prayer. I saw my parents kneeling at their bedside, whispering together their nightly Rosary. I saw old friends and neighbors singing hymns of veneration while walking through the fields for Marian processions. The savior of my priesthood, Fr. Balley, was set always before my imagination, where I watched him reach for Jesus-in-the-Host with arthritic fingers and stretch his arms and Jesus toward the arches of his parish. I saw my deceased soldier-brother Francis beseeching God's protection as bullets hurtled toward him. I saw the pale faces of holy priests huddled in prayer, the ones long dead who had hidden in my family's barn to escape the guillotine. I saw myself as an eight-year-old in a meadow leading my shepherd friends in the Angelus. And I saw myself preaching a little sermon to the shepherds, perched behind my invisible ambo on a haystack. Ah, what wonderful consolations these images of prayer gave me.

Dear reader, it is from these memories of prayer—and listening to God for ways to shepherd Ars—that I urge you to increase the measure of your meditative prayer. It was this type of intimate union with God that helped me pry open the doors of even Ars's most hardened souls. I am your coach, but I am also a shepherd *in persona Christi*—so I must enlighten you to a rather embarrassing memory of what the Reign of Terror did to disfigure the face of the Catholic Church in France.

The harrowing reality of what I came to see as "bachelor priesthoods" came into view as I walked the countryside to introduce myself to the pastors of Ars's neighboring parishes. I knocked on presbytery doors and was greeted by what seemed to be bored or even bothered pastors. The Revolution's murder of thousands of France's faithful priests and believers broke God's heart, but the hundreds of priests who denied him because of fear, I imagine, hurt nearly as much. These priests, who genuflected to Robespierre and then Napoleon, had forgotten the vows they had taken before the one true Emperor. They had forgotten their promise to God never to forsake saving souls.

When I saw the destruction of a prayer-less presbyterate in Trevoux, Villefranche-sur-Saône, Miserieux, and Sainte-Euphemie, I proclaimed to my parishioners: "Oh, how miserable is a priest who does not have a strong interior life."[21] The future of the Catholic faith in France was in peril then. As the sweet honeymoon of my priesthood died, I kept resting my head against Christ's heart in meditative prayer, where a single melody kept playing in my head: "We have this as a sure and steadfast anchor of the soul, a hope that enters into the inner shrine behind the curtain" (Heb 6:19).

This was a time when the walls came down and I began to see the Church as it was, rather than as I hoped it would be. Ecclesiastical traitors had been told by Revolutionary officials to diminish Christ's Gospel and replace it with tinny proclamations on tolerance, abiding love for Mother France, and a commitment to service over devotion. From behind ambos, the false priests rarely spoke of prayer. Perhaps worse, by their own lack of it, they never showed laity that prayer was necessary, the umbilical cord to God's sanctifying graces. The fallout of a prayer-less presbyterate was ruinous: the vast majority of once-fervent laity had fallen into vast spiritual malaise.

21. Saint Pierre, p. 161.

The malignancy of a devotion-less population had eroded the conscience of an entire nation.

This awareness, of course, sharpened and grew the sword in me. It marked the period in my life when I deeply intensified my prayer. My lifelong friend in Ars, Mademoiselle Lassagne, observed me in silent prayer then: "What a beautiful and edifying spectacle it was," she said.

> "To see [him] by the light of his candle, that figure emaciated by penances! He prayed with so much recollection! From time to time, he raised his eyes to the tabernacle, smiling so sweetly that one might have thought he beheld our Lord."[22]

Although I certainly had a peculiar visage, bystanders often shared with Mademoiselle Lassagne that my face became incandescent when I beheld the Eucharistic Face of Christ in the monstrance.

I daresay, dear reader, for the times in which you live, too, prayer must be wielded—as St. Michael the Archangel requested—as a weapon of war. Devoid of a consistent life of prayer, you are lacking the sword of the Spirit (the switchblade of zeal in your soul) that will enable you to parry Satan's attacks. And if you are not set right for these days of moral confusion, then your

22. Trochu, p. 341.

children and grandchildren will not be either. If, however, you stay united to God in daily and devoted prayer, you will not only find yourself with a heartbeat's chance of taming Satan—you will often find yourself conquering him.

Dear reader, I am removing my coaching cap for the remainder of this chapter. Until its final sentence and period at the end of it, I will write to you from my knees. Within the pages of this letter, this will be the only time I will *beg you.*

As your spiritual father in paradise, who saw the carnage of France, I see far more clearly today's ravages and wide-sweeping societal pain. I daresay, your need for a life of meditative prayer is as important now as at any time in the history of the world. *I beg you, I beg you, I beg you* to increase and intensify your prayers. The Teacher will never hide himself from the one who seeks him.

It is assumed, dear reader, the majority of you are Sunday Mass-goers, receive the sacraments, and spend time in prayer. Why, then, do I urge you to commit to greater amounts of interior prayer? For one, your children, grandchildren, and loved ones awaken each day to decadence and evil that surges into their souls. The Evil One has ensured that many children are no longer shocked by the images of unchecked sin flooding their screens. Do you not believe Satan works relentlessly through modern technology? Here is the worst-kept secret of our time: The cell phone has become Satan's most powerful tool, his demon in every pocket, the instrument he uses to dull young consciences and lure children toward a final, eternal separation from God.

The rise of dark ideologies, including Satanism, occultism, and witchcraft, has merged with the influence of secular modernism, contributing to the growing number of young adults who identify as Nones: holding no faith. Matthew quoted Jesus: "Let the children come to me, and do not hinder them; for to such belongs the kingdom of heaven" (Mt 19:14). Satan has often ripped Christ's words from the Gospel and turned them inside out. What were once considered some of Jesus's tenderest words today come off as a mocking hiss: *Let the children come to me, and do not hinder them—for my kingdom of hell belongs to such as these.*

Oh, how Our Lady mourns over the many children who seemed to have been orphaned by the world, and too often, by pastors. She weeps for one reason more than any other: Many fathers and mothers are asleep to the fog that pushes further each day into their children's souls. Mary sees Satan raging against young ones with few roadblocks. Far worse than sleeping parents, though, is the universe of parents who are aware of the poison but don't bother to guard their children against it.

My aim is not to alarm, but to save—so I will coach you now on a few methods of prayer. As God revealed to me in prayer what a spiritual father needed *to become* for Ars, it will be through deepening your prayer that wisdom, stamina, and graces will broaden in you. Prayer is the indestructible textile of union with God. In prayer you are instructed about how to shepherd your children—and shepherd your own soul while you're at it! The stakes are unmistakably high. For the first time, heaven sees the circumference of Earth split by a single wall. On one side, choruses of demons roam; on the other, willing saints try to contain them through lives of devoted prayer and striving for virtue. As I write these words, a worldwide technological revolution is hijacking the consciences of countless children—even your own—and it is your prayer and silent meditation on the life of Christ, dear reader, that will enable you to stand in the way.

Here is a path to contemplative prayer: When I was a new priest, I began to meditate on Jesus during his hidden years. Every day, I *saw* the Son of God at play, conversing with his Mother, working alongside Joseph, or walking the quiet paths of Nazareth. The images warmed my soul and taught me *to go light* as I embarked on my crusade to save Ars's souls. It will be soothing images such as these that will enable a lasting tranquility in you as you work to guard the children in your life, the wayward family members, friends, and neighbors.

I invite you to explore this way of meditative prayer. Perhaps start by building a small cell in your soul, fashioned to your own liking. You are in good company there; it was through contemplative prayer that Jesus united with his Father. It was in those far-off places that Jesus escaped the strains of the world and retreated into the warmth of his Father's love. My own inner cell was simple; it was a small parlor in an inn, where two wooden benches rested by a warming fire. A teapot always simmered by the hearth fire, beneath an image of the Sacred Heart. All was quiet in the half-light. It was there, in the thatch cottage in my soul, that Jesus in his hidden years emerged, awaiting me on the bench across from mine. It was there we spoke, heart to heart, without ever opening our mouths. It was this contemplative way that calmed me and gave me the wisdom and direction I lacked as a new priest.

The good Lord knows the many anxieties, dilemmas, and distractions that invade your life. God's burning desire is to shepherd you through your trials, inviting you to find his yoke through meditative prayer. He knows the weight of your daily tasks and the many duties that fill your hours, and he understands that you cannot walk away from them. Yet, still, he calls you to seek him in the midst of your life. In those quiet moments, when you pause—if only for a brief instant—to turn your heart toward him, his grace has the power to lighten your burdens and guide you through.

I stand firm on this: There are no excuses for not rising early to speak with God. When you begin your day in contemplative prayer, you'll feel something like a pilot light blink to life within your soul. As you continue to spend time in his presence, that small flicker often grows into a flame, gradually warming every part of you. This feeling is the action of Christ pouring into you. Because of this early-morning experience of peace, comfort, and enlightenment, you might soon find yourself wanting to reenter the warmth of the hermitage of your prayer at various points of the day. That is what happens when you have come to know that the Trinity's all-consuming love awaits you there.

These secret visits to your soul are like precious cargo set before the heart of God, who responds to your generosity by bestowing resilience, humility, clarity, and peace of mind in you as you go about your day. This little hermitage of secret encounter with God can't help but change everything in your life. Why? Because your inner cell has become a palace of deep friendship with your Savior, whose love consumes you.

With meditative prayer, you will be a presence of lasting light in the world. Even strangers will see a supernatural charity, joy, and hope in you. The world will also see, in a way they may not understand, the fullness of Truth. Your loved ones will observe that you carry yourself lighter, differently—and they will want what you have unknowingly given them. All of this will take place because you've spent more time with God in devotion. I once said of prayer:

> "Through prayer we receive a foretaste of heaven and something of paradise comes down upon us. Prayer never leaves us without sweetness. It is honey that flows into the soul and makes all things sweet. When we pray properly, sorrows disappear like snow before the sun."[23]

Just as God commissioned the apostles to carry the Good News to an unknowing world, he has nourished you through prayer so that you, too, can become his ambassador. In a rather simple way, it is a sacred four-step process:

1. God inspires you to meet him in the quiet of your soul.
2. By obliging, you abide with him.
3. In the loving depths of relationship, you are able to discern his holy will.

23. Lopez.

4. He sends you out as his missionary to radiate his love to your family, loved ones, and world.

This is the simple way of heaven's umbilical cord. Because of worldliness, humanity often disregards the lifeline of prayer because they cannot *see it* or how it might help them. Too many simply have not heard from clergy of the necessity of meditative prayer.

The consequence of a poor prayer life is grave, in the same way it is for the underdeveloped child in the womb suffering the effects of a malnourished mother. When the umbilical cord between God and man is cut—*or never even activated*—the powers and principalities quickly feed on the empty soul. Thereafter, in slow motion, people become zombie-like figures driven to whatever their flesh desires. Nonpraying souls wound God terribly. Matthew, Mark, Luke, and John took up their reed pens and recorded on parchment the perfect example of prayer, capturing what they witnessed in Christ, who sought his Father in solitary, lonesome, and secluded places. More than any other reason, souls are lost to hell because they did not pray.

In time, all of Ars returned to the Mass and the sacraments. I now know that had I not kept retreating to Jesus in prayer before the tabernacle, these poor souls would not have been shepherded back. Millions upon millions of today's lost souls do not return to God because they do not pray.

Dear reader, each of you knows of a loved one who has left the sacraments. God yearns for willing shepherds to lead them back. But more and more, God looks to *you*. Heaven collectively holds its breath and looks lovingly upon *you* when you wade into a conversation with one who has left the Faith. God sees you enter the ebb tide of a lost lamb's worldly thoughts and rebuttals. He sees your conversations becoming awkward and disjointed, notwithstanding that you spent a great amount of time in prayer beforehand. He would have me tell you that it's acceptable to ask the lamb why he or she has left the Faith. He wants you to ask if you can pray for them, or if you can pick them up for Sunday Mass.

We know that too often these lambs reject your invitations. But as your coach, I urge you from the sidelines of your soul to keep fighting to find creative ways to pray for your lost loved ones and to speak of God's never-ending love for them. Keep extending unobtrusive invitations, prayers, and penances as you surrender the prodigal son or daughter to God's care. He loves your lost ones far more than you do.

Lastly, as the saints discussed in heaven earlier in this letter, there are not enough shepherds to herd the masses of today's wandering sheep. You are vital participants in saving their souls. St. Monica's long years of prayer for Augustine's conversion rose to heaven like lyric verses of poems, groans, and unbreakable love letters of trust. In time, God gave her St. Ambrose to penetrate the hardness of her son's heart. God has a stable of witnesses just as powerful as Ambrose. He has endless storehouses of divine means to bring lost ones back— and you, my dear friend, are one of them.

A Thought on Prayer

I once said, "God commands you to pray, but he forbids you to worry."[24] *If I didn't devote myself to prayer in Ars, my many worries would have prevented the town's conversion, for I would not have been truly free to hear and obey God's promptings.*

- Meditate upon Christ's words in Matthew 6:25–34.
- What things in your life cause you to become anxious and worried?
- Can you recognize, perhaps through a personal experience, how worry leads to a lack of freedom to listen, hear, and act upon God's will? What are practical ways that you can relieve yourself of worry?

24. Brandon Vogt, "Learning from a Priest Who Converted a Town," Brandon Vogt's website, https://brandonvogt.com/learning-priest-converted-town/.

- When you find yourself becoming anxious, immediately invite God to come into that uneasy place and to bring healing. Speak in prayer to him until the anxiety dissipates.
- If you do not spend time in meditative prayer, begin to build a cell in your soul to meet God. Fashion it to your liking: Make it the most beautiful and peaceful place in the world to grow in friendship with God.

The relic of the incorrupt heart of St. John Vianney, kept in a sanctuary at his shrine in Ars, France. His heart has also been displayed in other locations as part of national pilgrimages.

Chapter 4

Your Need for a Demanding Queen

(Repeating Mary's Yes)

The price of Ars beginning a slow return to grace was a matter of give-and-take. If a long-wandering soul crossed the threshold of my confessional, the Evil One's work to subtract from me intensified. As I tried to sleep, my body became the penitent's ransom.

Grappin's infestations became a routine part of my life, mostly at night. Villagers came to regard my presbytery as a haunted house. Many overheard the malignant spirit's physical attacks, vomitings, moans, and wicked laughter. Some nights, some reported seeing my rectory shake as it emitted otherworldly sounds. My bedroom became a chilling repository of echoes: locomotives, swinging sledgehammers, swarms of hornets, slamming doors, splitting wood, and thundering teams of horses racing up my stairwell. "I came to the conclusion that it was the devil because I was afraid. The good God does not frighten us,"[25] I said. I told a friend of the nights the devil sang from my fireplace like a haunted nightingale. Some saw blood on the walls and pieces of steel shrapnel on the floor. A pair of guards, who agreed to investigate the phenomena, fled my presbytery in horror that same night and never returned. I shared with Mademoiselle Lassagne that Grappin told me he was going to kill me. But mostly, he just pulled me from my bed and violently threw me to the floor. He did, though, set fire to my bed one night. "The villainous Grappin," I said. "He could not catch the bird, so he burns the cage."[26]

Thankfully, though, Grappin was stupid. I began to understand his wiles as a matter of mathematics. When there was a spike in vexations, I realized a long-lost soul, or several sinners in need of absolution, were walking the path to Ars. So, as Grappin puffed like a bull and his harassments worsened, I grit my teeth for another sleepless night to prepare for "the good haul of fish"[27] I

25. Trochu, p. 255.

26. Fr. Bartholomew J. O'Brien, "The Devil Came to Ars," TAN-Direction, https://tandirection.com/pursuit-of-perfection/the-devil-came-to-ars/.

27. Trochu, p. 255.

knew was coming to my confessional after the break of dawn.

As townsfolk saw me as a country pastor who fought the devil for them, my parish began to grow a bit—although many recalcitrant sinners still stayed far from me and the sacraments. In a way, these lost souls saw *me* as the diabolic oppressor of Ars. Because I proclaimed clearly and unapologetically that repeated sins of drunken promiscuity would damn them to hell, tavern owners, gamblers, the bawdy cabaret set, and their rowdy and lustful clientele awarded me the number one spot on the list of troublemakers in the entire Auvergne-Rhône-Alpes region. As gossip, lies, and mudslinging became the norm, Grappin seemed to have suddenly become a secondary problem. These attackers harassed me nearly as powerfully as the company of demons. I was told by close friends that I was being called neurotic, a hypocrite, and was even accused of fathering a child. At least Grappin had the courtesy to rage in the open; this set slunk around and whispered.

I begged God then to give me the grace to stay above the maliciousness and perjury, but there were days when I grew lonely. Rumbling storm clouds of hopelessness sometimes passed through me when I considered the level of sin and inhumanity, and how evil so easily overpowered my efforts to help heal Ars.

My sadness soon gave way to anxiety, and even heartbreak, when those newly sacramentalized at Ars—and even a few of the Mass-going faithful at St. Sixtus—remained silent bystanders as my character was torn apart. I imagine it was fear that prevented them from defending my name—and responding with stories of how my pastoral care and sacrifices helped lead them back to Christ. I also noticed, though, that Grappin had reoriented his strategy. To cut off the piecemeal spiritual renewal of Ars and to lay waste to my priesthood, he, too, began to whisper rather than rage—purring lies and thorns of doubt about me into my flock's ears. The centerpiece of his attacks rested on the manner of my preaching: *This hateful man cuts like a knife from the pulpit; his severity is purposeful in demoralizing you. You are meant for heaven; it is this sick man who casts you to hell.* The Evil One's revised tactic of whispering to my flock's still-shiftless conscience began to peel away Sunday Mass-goers. Some friends turned their heads or gave cold looks when I passed by. In time, a walk through town felt like stepping to the end of a gangplank.

Satan seemed to be winning, and forsakenness snaked around my soul. My dear mother and father, siblings, Fr. Balley, and childhood friends were either dead or far away. It became clear one brokenhearted night in my presbytery that outside of God and the heavenly court, I was detached from all my loved ones on earth. Grappin whispered to my flock, but at nights in my bedroom he mocked me polyphonically. On the especially raucous nights, I'd leave the presbytery to pray. As I plodded over to the refuge of St. Sixtus, the burlesque show's hoots, banging piano, and gin-soaked vulgarities managed to turn Ars's gentle moonlit night into the skies above Gethsemane. A malevolent force trailed me, becoming Goliath-like in its taunts: *You will never change them, because you cannot stop us from destroying their minds.*

I always kept a single candle by my parish's small statue of Mary. Tears often sprang to my eyes as I knelt before her image and poured out to my Mother my grief over the power of Satan. Some nights I sobbed, and found myself unable to pray even a single *Ave*. My mind always eased, though, when I reached my hand to her tiny foot and rested it there, knowing how it snapped Satan's neck. I pleaded over and over, *My Queen—Mother me now. . . . My Queen, Mother me now*. Thereafter, the grip of powerlessness loosened and was replaced by a languorous ribbon of peace. My mental riot evaporated into thin air as an all-encompassing maternal warmth covered me.

But in the silence—and in the core of my soul—Mary spoke jarring words to me: *Jean-Marie, nail yourself to my Son's Cross. Until you surrender everything to God, even Satan's attacks, you cannot resemble my Son, and Ars cannot be healed. Your acceptance and patient resignation to the calumnies, alienation, and harassments are the matchsticks that will set Ars aflame for love of my Son.* Dear reader, the Queen had given me the secret: there *had* to be a cost to surrendering everything to God to bring Ars back to a place of grace. I had to learn to suffer in the same fashion as the unloved, abandoned, and tortured Christ.

Thereafter, I no longer regarded Mary as I did after leaving the crib in Dardilly. Where once she was a soft blaze of peace and maternal gentleness for me, Mary now spoke to my soul as the queen and commander of all of heaven's angels, each of whom bowed to her before engaging with the demons. She continually pointed me to the crucified priesthood I had promised her Son.

I began to meditate on the Sorrowful Mysteries of the Rosary differently then. Mary took me by the hand, decade-by-decade, into the savagery of what she saw after Jesus left Gethsemane. I saw her evince her motherhood through courage and resolve. Despite the barbarity of the soldiers, mocking Jewish leaders, and risk to her own life, Mary knelt in the mud to watch her Son slowly die on the Cross. She showed me what a Mother of Sorrows is and does. She wasn't just a weeping mother, she was an indomitable force who saw, heard, and viscerally felt the heaving of her Son's tortured breaths. Still, she refused to take her eyes off of him. She walked every step of his blood trail, enduring his passion until the end, when she fused her mortified heart with his.

I'd like to share a stunning little story that has been passed around paradise. As has been memorialized in the Stations of the Cross, there was a moment when Jesus fell hard to the ground as he processed up Golgotha. As he writhed beneath the weight of the Cross, with blood from the crown of thorns blurring his eyes, he made out the image of his ringed-eyed Mother, kneeling before him horrified by his bloodstained body. After looking penetratingly into her Son's eyes, she thrust out her arms—for the Cross. *Son, you must finish this.* As Jesus slowly rose from the ground, Mary stood with her arms wrapped around the Cross. This holy woman was the Mother of God, too—and this plan of salvation needed to be consummated. Demons were startled then; it marked the moment their lost souls were first besieged by fear of her. Their terror has grown.

Dear reader, I imagine the majority of you are devoted to Our Lady—but do you ever consider her potency? On your most frightful days and nights—when diabolic pokes harass you—do you call to her? Each of you has likely, in some fashion, felt seemingly otherworldly harassments. Why would you hold back from pleading for Mary's aid, since the demons scatter at the mention of her name? There is a reason Marian statuary often shows one of her calloused feet breaking the neck of Satan—because from the beginning to the end, Mary said "yes" to God's plan. When sin, pain, and disorder shot into the world at Satan's successful tempting of Adam and Eve, God promised a Redeemer: "I will put enmity between you and the woman, and between your seed and her seed; he shall bruise your head, and you shall bruise his heel" (Gn 3:15). The Woman kills the serpent *through her seed.*

When flood tides of panic over Ars's slanderers and fading parishioners merged with lewd images of the drunken liaisons of poor young souls, it was Mary who *pushed me* through, reminding me of the Cross her Son carried. When I imagined Ars's souls burning in hell, she simply redirected me to the priestly sacrifices and tasks that would save them. When I mourned over Satan's tireless whispers and attacks, she reminded me of how her Son handled him in the desert. Always, Mary exhorted me to become like her Son, while reminding me of my identity as an immovable shepherd of souls.

I said in a sermon around that time:

> If you invoke the Blessed Virgin when you are tempted [to despair], she will come at once to your help, and Satan will leave you. . . .
>
> The most Holy Virgin places herself between her Son and us. The greater sinners we are, the more tenderness and compassion does she feel for us.

> The child that has cost its mother most tears is the dearest to her heart. Does not a mother always run to the help of the weakest and the most exposed to danger? Is not a physician in the hospital most attentive to those who are most seriously ill? The Heart of Mary is so tender towards us, that those of all the mothers in the world put together are like a piece of ice in comparison to hers.[28]

In 1836, I consecrated my parish to Mary under the title of the Immaculate Conception. Shortly thereafter, I had a bronzed heart crafted to hold the names of all the parishioners of Ars, written on a white silk ribbon. Even now, that heart is suspended from the neck of the statue of the Virgin in Ars.

Dear mothers and fathers, dear faithful disciples, I implore you to invoke the Blessed Virgin and place your children and loved ones within her Immaculate Heart. But remember, you must also be active participants in Our Lady's work. Just as Mary, in a sense, nailed herself to her Son's Cross by sharing in his agony, she calls you to enter into your children's hidden and often unspoken pains, into the secret sorrows of your friends and neighbors. If your children have strayed from the Faith, she expects you to nail your doubts, your pain, and your uncertainty

28. Ray Sullivan, "The Wisdom of a Super-Saint, St. John Vianney," The Catholic Stand, April 18, 2022, https://catholicstand.com/the-wisdom-of-a-super-saint-st-john-vianney/.

about their return to the Cross—trusting fully that her Son will find them and bring them back to the fold. She begs you to play an active role in Christ's rescue mission. She calls you to make sacrifices: to commit to fasts, penances, Rosaries, and unceasing acts of love for your lost ones. You must help her Son save them.

As you set up your manger scene this Christmas, do not regard Mary as a blue-robed, easily broken porcelain doll. She was not a silent bystander to God's plan for salvation; she was handpicked by God from the beginning of time to love, guard, and help guide her Son in his humanity. Because Mary was unstained by Original Sin, her intellect was unlike anyone born of woman, save her Son. There is nothing dainty about what Mary expects from you as you work to guide your children through a moral winter. She will press you to keep ahead of the pace of the spreading ideologies and to remain holy, sacrificial, and hardworking for your children, but also for your spouse, friend, and coworker, too. Our Lady does not permit many respites. As she *pushed herself* over countless hills to reach Elizabeth, thoughts of her resilience will help drive you from bed each morning to fight for her Son and to proclaim the Good News whenever it is possible.

Beneath her eyelids, closed in prayer, are eyes that blaze with expectation for you. Your sacrifices, toil, and small martyrdoms for your children and loved ones are precisely analogous to the inexhaustible *yeses* Mary offered to God until her Dormition in Ephesus. It is Mary's ribbon of *yeses* that will serve as your still point and example on those days when you are weary. And when Mary sees you rise above your exhaustion and pain to pour out demonstrations of love, she will become perhaps your greatest intercessor, and say to her Son: *Jesus, send to this persevering one your graces.*

The greatest saints experienced firsthand the magnificent work done in them through Mary's hand. Bernard of Clairvaux, Bonaventure, John Damascene, Louis de Montfort, Alphonse Liguori, Francis of Assisi, John Paul, and countless others gave their entire lives to Mary. The symmetry of their understanding of Mary was simple. As Jesus revealed at the wedding feast in Cana, he can never reject a plea from his sinless Mother. These two thousand years later, nothing has changed. I once spoke of this relationship:

> The heart of this good Mother is all love and mercy; she desires only to see us happy. We have only to turn to her to be heard. The Son has his justice, the Mother has nothing but her love. Her Son, being ready to punish a sinner—Mary interposes, checks the sword, implores pardon for the poor criminal. "Mother," Our Lord says to her, "I can refuse you

> nothing. If Hell could repent, you would obtain its pardon."[29]

As you awaken each day into the rising tide of growing godlessness, I beg you to plead for Mary's intercessory aid. Remember what St. Bonaventure said: "Men do not fear a powerful hostile army as the powers of hell fear the name and protection of Mary."[30] While it is true that Mary pondered all things in her heart, she had a heart that spilled over with the same visceral passion of John the Baptist. It goes unmentioned in the Acts of the Apostles, but Mary was weary of the behavior of Christ's apostles at Pentecost. She knew that even after three years of absorbing her Son's many miracles and seeing him in the flesh after the Resurrection, many had returned to their former ways of life. When the Spirit descended in the Upper Room that day, Mary's eyes became flames of demand. It's a little laugh line in heaven: The apostles scattered to all corners of the earth just to flee from Mary!

Perhaps dear reader, it is unsettling for you to see Mary in her warlike stance, but it is exactly this posture that is necessary to counter Satan on behalf of your lost loved

---

29. "St. John Vianney Speaks on the Blessed Virgin Mary," *The Marian Room,* August 9, 2019, https://themarianroom.com/st-john-vianney-speaks-on-the-blessed-virgin-mary/.

30. Quote by St. Bonaventure, My Catholic Prayers, https://mycatholicprayers.com/quotes/men-do-not-fear-a-powerful-hostile-army-as-the-powers-of-hell-fear-the-name-and-protection-of-mary/.

ones. As Mary repeatedly squared her shoulders against challenges, and even the dragon, she invites you to do your best each day to tame today's multiheaded serpents. All Mary ever was, and all she ever can be, is one who points to the saving work of her Son and the demands he places on you to become his disciple in a society that will often hate you for it.

Mary's heart beats to bring humanity to the embrace of her Son. But until he returns, the devil will rage against that lasting embrace. So how do we end these thoughts on Our Lady? Perhaps by echoing what she might encourage you in this hour: *My Son died to save the lost ones—and you must die, too.*

A Thought On Mary

I once noticed a charming event that helped lead to Ars's conversion. When I prayed the Rosary on walks through my parish boundaries, even hard-nosed farmers stopped working in the fields to pay respect to my devotion to my Mother.

- Meditate upon Mary's song of praise in Luke 1:46–55.
- What does it mean to you to "magnify the Lord" and what do you think this meant to Mary? How can you magnify the Lord throughout your day, and witness Mary's strength and resolve for the lost loved ones in your life?

- Do you pray the Rosary every day, as Mary requested? If not, why not? What keeps you from this devotion to Our Lady?

- Ask Mary to help you love the Rosary, to find in it a comfort and salve in this "valley of tears," in which you can unite yourself to Christ and his life's mysteries. As you pray the Rosary, imagine yourself and those who have fallen from the Faith wrapped up in her loving mantle, protected and guided, teaching you—and her Son's lost lambs—how to reunite with and return to him.

These are the images of saints that hung on Vianney's bedroom wall. From left to right, top row: St. Vincent DePaul, Our Lady of the Immaculate Conception, Jesus at the Last Summer, St. John the Baptist baptizing Jesus. Bottom row: St. John the Baptist, St. Philomena, Our Lady's Assumption, a reliquary.

Chapter 5

The Fight Within and Without

(Fortitude: The Muscle of Your Virtue)

The temptation to flee Ars for "God alone" was the thorn of my priesthood. Despite giving my life to God to become a pastor of souls, I fled my identity three times to seek solitude as a Trappist. But even as I beat moonlit paths away from the burden of my duty, my conscience flared: *Judas, why do you abandon your flock; why do you desert their souls?* Shattered by my humiliation, I soon found myself absolving sin back at St. Sixtus as morning rays stretched into Ars.

Now in paradise, I know many of the souls in Ars would have been damned if I had received safe passport into a cloister. I also know the special train line to Lyons wouldn't have existed, which would have meant tens of thousands of French and European visitors who traveled to seek my absolution could have died in sin. Arctic winds blow through my soul when I consider the eternal repercussions of what my desertion of God and souls would have done had I selfishly left Ars behind to become a monk.

A single choice, knowingly made against one's conscience, has given birth to history's greatest monsters. Christ said: "Let what you say be simply 'Yes' or 'No'; anything more than this comes from evil" (Mt 5:37). These "yes" and "no" choices begin in the soul. Sadly, today's growing ignorance or rejection of the conscience has become one of the greatest sorrows in heaven.

In paradise, I have come to know the great John Henry Newman, the British convert and former leader of the Anglican Oxford Movement. I once overheard the holy intellectual explaining to a company of saints the reason he had chosen the term "the aboriginal Vicar of Christ" to describe the conscience. In a voice rich with a melodic, High-Anglican pitch, he said, *Ah, so many have puzzled over this expression!* Newman bellowed, his words echoing with the clarity of truth: *The task of the Vicar—the St. Peter that resides within our souls—is to guide us, and to actually authorize us to make wise and holy choices.*

It is this inner voice—our inner compass—that orders our thoughts, desires, and actions to God, bringing us into alignment with his will.

He paused for a moment, his expression reflective, before adding, *I must confess that my own theology of conscience emerged from my own journey—from Anglicanism to the refulgence of the pilgrim faith. Even though I knew that my decision could mean total rejection by the Church of England, my inner Vicar whispered, "John, if it is true, you must go." And so, I went home.*

Never in history has there been a greater need for models with the native strength of Newman, who in obeying his conscience accepted the antipathy and total rejection of most everyone he knew and once held dear. Conversely, millions of Catholics today hear the same inner whispers Newman did—to share the fullness of the Catholic faith with fallen-away family members, friends, and coworkers—but they stay mute. Self-preservation, fear, unease, societal courtesy, or some other rationalization drowns out the voice of their Vicar. It is Christians' refusal to boldly proclaim Christ and the gospel to unbelievers that wounds God and heaven's saints more than any other omission. It is the scandal of modern Catholicism. Because of his own formerly scarred conscience, the tax collector, sinner, and convert Matthew was clear on the matter when he quoted the God-Man for whom he left everything behind: "Whoever denies me before men, I also will deny before my Father who is in heaven" (Mt 10:33).

God has asked that I coach, and not frighten, you. But dear reader, at this point in my letter, you no longer need to be gently fed with milk. It is impossible to be gentle about the consequences of what the widening crisis of malformed or ignored consciences has done in America and beyond, and the manner in which the erosion of reason has unraveled the fabric of the West. Perhaps an intimate look might help you to see the devastation at the rise of the moon each night in these spiritually bereft, haunted houses.

Allow me to pull back the heavy drapes and escort you through the front door of a single American home. I never softened the edges of sin from my pulpit, and I won't now. I reveal it so that it might scare *you* straight, if, in fact, you need to be. A chilling symphony streams toward heaven each night, a discordant chorus of hideous laughter and groans that alerts the heavenly court to the harrowing scene set to unfold. (Voluminous books could be written on the reasons for Mary's agony, but the following scene is perhaps her greatest sorrow.) A pure soul—a small child, adolescent, or teenager—is behind a locked bedroom door scrolling on a phone. A demon lies in wait. Aware of his malevolence, an angel pleads for the child he's been tasked to guard, but the demon's wiles are too finely honed.

In time, it comes—an image of carnality that bursts onto the screen in a rush of sensory overload that shocks the helpless child's system. The child has never before imagined such an image. With emotions stirred and riotous—and with his or her conscience still unformed—the demon goads the child more intensely to the image, where he or she becomes trapped like an eel in a barrel. The spiraling begins. The innocent child is now in the demon's lair, where—horrifically—he or she will often, much later in life, become a slave to sin. Because the demon has endless cabinets of wiles, he will occasionally harass the child through a classmate's text-message bullying, or rely on an invitation from a trafficker to induce the child to meet at the mall food court over the weekend. Other times, he'll slow-walk a boy or girl into an addiction to TikTok, Snapchat, or another site that works to numb a pure soul that months earlier was an image of bright-eyed wonder and joy.

But dear reader, permit me to draw back the drapery even further. This diabolic crushing of purity unfolds with dads and moms often down the hallway, where they, too, are often scrolling. As Satan presses deeper into the young one's mind, parents are often melding with "friends" on social media streams. On any given night—

for example—paradise might see a mother choosing to pick a fight against a political or religious opponent, or flexing her maternity by fighting for Mother Earth, a hunted lion on the Ivory Coast, or wholesale acceptance of a woman's choice to do anything and everything to which she's inclined. Although it is mostly like-minded friends who view her posts, the rarely-if-ever-to-be-seen-in-person "friends" tap out quick "attagirls" and push red hearts and thumbs-up emojis that energizes the mother with a dose of dopamine. While savoring the approval of her activism, she forgets about her husband in the next room who is scrolling through sites that granularly break down statistics of players on his favorite football team. Or perhaps he is leisurely scrolling through pornographic images while listening to a favorite podcast host who always "gets it right." This home is eerily quiet; there is only the background drone of the television. The only sounds *heard* are from the voice inside their cell phones that subliminally whispers: *Stay with me, just a bit longer.* The voice is why so many Catholics no longer bother with the voice of their *Vicar*; they've allowed it to be annihilated, drowned out by the embrace of their self-tailored technological choruses of demons.

This is the Western anti–fairy tale heaven sees. The details, of course, vary from home to home, but these images are not apocryphal. Entire homes become commandeered by the Beast, who has hardly had to move a talon. These overtakings move each night like World War I chlorine gases into unguarded souls, unseen, with hardly a word, movement, or objection from a parent or guardian.

It is the crisis of your times.

Dear reader, is it a wonder why there is disorder in your nation and world today? My friend Newman prophesied more than a century ago about the haunting phenomena of the diminished conscience in comfortable homes. He said,

> I observe that a civilized age is more exposed to subtle sins than a rude age. Why? For this simple reason, because it is more fertile in excuses and evasions. It can defend error, and hence can blind the eyes of those who have not very careful consciences. It can make error plausible, it can make vice look like virtue. It dignifies sin by fine names; it calls avarice proper care of one's family.[31]

Glory be to God, my conscience sent me back to Ars after my temporary abandonment of my spiritual children. Although many today have suppressed, reengineered, or badly wounded their conscience, any honest parent will

31. Fr. Piotr Olszanowski, "Newman's Concept of Conscience in His Quest for Moral Truth," *Homiletic and Pastoral Review*, February 10, 2020, https://www.hprweb.com/2020/02/newmans-concept-of-conscience-in-his-quest-for-moral-truth/.

admit they are periodically alerted to how their comfort has sometimes made them "less of a parent." Put in a different and more indelicate way, their embrace of sloth has prevented them from properly caring for their child. An eroded conscience, for example, might tell a parent their habit of scrolling is a reward and justifiable way of unwinding after a long day. In their innermost recesses, though—when they engage their conscience—many know it is laziness that keeps them from parenting their child. St. Thomas Aquinas said the vice of sloth was an enslavement to worldly comfort that led men to withdraw from good due to the sorrow of lacking pleasure.

My own conscience steered me through my unbloody war to choose the moral right and harder path in Ars. How I fared in obliging my conscience, I knew, would be the determinant of the efficacy of my priesthood. But it was far deeper; how I responded to my conscience dictated my eternal fate, or at the very least, shaped the degree and proportion of my purification.

But let us move on from this deadly vice of sloth to coach you to its opposite. Let me write now of the oft-forgotten cardinal virtue of fortitude. Although biographers have written extensively on my care of souls, few have turned over rocks or drilled deep into me to uncover what fueled my burning love for souls. It certainly didn't fall from out of the sky; it had to be "won over" by the numerous choices I made. These daily choices regulated my level of sacrifice, piety, magnanimity, prayerfulness, and vigilance. Through God's grace and cooperation with the Holy Spirit, the choices I made mapped the course of my entire life. Because the devil knew I wanted to live in harmony with my conscience, he relentlessly tempted me to become lazy. Even still, Grappin wasn't my greatest threat—the threat was *me*. I hungered to live the eremitic life, and often awakened with an intense desire to leave Ars forever. With this knowledge, Grappin began his unending whisper campaign: *You deserve it John*, he whispered in his kindest way. *You are God's unique one. He knows of your love for prayer.* I had to fight his lie—and my desire for solitude—with a single refrain: *Dear Lord, keep me firm in my duty to shepherd Ars; stiffen my resolve.*

Fortitude was the unshakable foundation of my priesthood. In the words of the *Catechism of the Catholic Church,* this virtue "ensures firmness in difficulties and constancy in the pursuit of the good. . . . It disposes one even to renounce and sacrifice his life in defense of a just cause."[32] Neither the priesthood nor the parenting of a child nor even the faithful living of the Christian life in any circumstance is for the faint of heart. When I was tempted to the "self-care" of napping, sleeping in,

32. *Catechism of the Catholic Church*, 2nd ed. (Libreria Editrice Vaticana–United States Conference of Catholic Bishops, 2000), no. 1808.

lessening my availability for confessions, or skipping a catechism class at *La Providence*, I quickly summoned to mind Christ's three years of tireless public ministry. But it was his passion and embrace of his identity on the Cross that became my indelible model of fortitude.

I was also abundantly blessed with warm memories of my two greatest earthly models of perseverance, my parents, Matthieu and Marie, whose unfaltering sacrifice carved icons of stamina into my soul. I want to draw you back to the days when my identity was forged—when through the witness of their fortitude, my parents showed me that substantial obstacles could be overcome through grit and God's mercy and grace. They centered their lives around making holy and hard choices. Their conscience directed them, but it was their vigilance to see their decisions through that made them holy.

Although my father explained to me as a boy that I was growing up at a difficult time, he didn't tell me he was raising me on farmland irrigated by the blood of martyrs. A few of his priest friends, who served at parishes within a few kilometers of our home, had their heads removed for refusing to sign the oath of allegiance to Robespierre. I never knew the priests living in our barn were in hiding. Their refusal to serve as false priests for the Revolution made them fugitives, hunted men. Still, my father knew he needed to risk his own life to save the lives of these holy men. As I grew, I began to understand why my father frequently took the time to teach me about the responsibilities and demands of manhood. He explained a man's burden by telling me stories of the masculinity of Christ. He said a man must be willing to confront and rebuke ill-intentioned "white-washed tombs," even at the risk of his life. He was showing me images of the crosses I would one day have to embrace each day of my life.

One Sunday morning we turned in the opposite direction of our parish and walked a few hours into the countryside for what was my first barn Mass. Sadness shone in my parents' eyes throughout that strange day. They didn't tell me our pastor, Fr. James Rey[33]—whom my parents invited into our home for meals—had not stayed true to God. He signed the oath to the Revolution. Oh, poor Fr. Rey—he lacked the virtue of fortitude; he feared death more than the fate of his soul, and as I write, Fr. Rey is paying the price. My father began speaking to me on a deeper level then: *Jean-Marie, we go to where God is, even if the entire world goes the other direction.*

My mother gave me what would become my most treasured gift. Even on my deathbed, I spoke of the small wooden statue of Mary that I carried with me everywhere. In the turmoil of the godless Revolution,

33. Saint Pierre, p. 6.

my mother understood that I needed a deeper, more enduring form of motherly love. She knew that suffering would be my companion, and so, her gift of the statue was her way of binding me to the woman who had, with unyielding resolve, raised the Son of God. My mother recognized that the strength and courage Mary displayed on Golgotha would serve like a catechism on fortitude. That little statue became my compass. Each night, when I placed it on my bedside table, it shone like a nightlight that scattered demons and set the peace of the newborn babe into my soul.

My friends good-naturedly began to tease that my statue was glued to me, and it began to serve me like a Bible. I often held her statue and pointed to her visage when I "preached" to my friends as we shepherded our flocks in the valley of Chante-Merle. *We must climb the same hill Mary did,* I proclaimed from atop my haystack. *Mary never abandoned her Son. We mustn't either.* I didn't know then that I was preaching on the virtue of fortitude. As the monstrosities of the Reign of Terror became clearer, I encouraged my friends to orient themselves entirely to Mary at the Cross, so we could be fully united to Jesus in preparation for any dark days ahead. Thankfully, I preached the message into my own heart—because obstacles and crosses mounted.

As a teenager, I was often teased for my eccentricities, my small stature, and my indifference to my studies. The more our family grew, the deeper our poverty became. While Robespierre was undeniably evil, his successor, the atheist Napoleon, proved nearly as harmful. My days were consumed with long hours of labor on the farm, and by the time I turned seventeen, my education was almost nonexistent.

Although I had always longed to become a priest, my father, for years, was sternly against it. He said I was needed as a farmhand. When he finally relented and I began seminary studies, I struggled from the start. I could not pass a single Latin class. My poor head wouldn't allow me to memorize even the Scripture passages I held dear in my heart. I became known as the dunce of minor seminary, a hopeless case to which my rector in Verrières gave the grade of "very weak" in theology before he kicked me out in 1813. I would be dismissed two more times for poor grades, until by the grace of God, I was readmitted. I often thought then: How does one become a channel of grace for souls when he's unable to grasp even a single abstract theological thought?

Ah, for the gift of grit—the virtue of fortitude. I never stopped believing God would intervene in my trials. Mom and Dad showed on the farm that obstacles were meant to be overcome, not dwelled upon. I knew

God had planted an untamed desire in me to turn over my life to him as a priest—so I fought for this dream, no matter how dim it became. I kept to my tortured studies, took on penances, stayed devoted to prayer, and stayed true to whatever the holy Fr. Balley encouraged. After the good pastor invited me into his "home-school seminary" in the neighboring village of Écully, he told me that a patient acceptance of the cross of my intellectual frailties would one day produce harvests of gold for souls. He assuaged the doubts of skeptical seminary formators by explaining that my "uniqueness" was a gift that strengthened my faith and crushed every thread of pride. He told them my love for God was unlike any seminarian he had ever known. After winning the argument, the holy Fr. Balley told me he wouldn't quit on me if I didn't quit on myself.

It was a hot Wednesday afternoon on July 9, 1815—just days after the pounding of Napoleon's army at the Battle of Waterloo—when Fr. Philippe Courbon, the vicar general acting on behalf of the archbishop, installed me as a Roman Catholic priest in the Archdiocese of Lyons. Citing my piety, devotion to Mary, and the willingness I'd shown in seminary to shepherd souls, Fr. Courbon said of me: "The Church is in need of not only learned priests; she wants, above all, holy priests."[34] At the age of twenty-nine, after a steady stream of failures, rejections, and uncertainties, I began to pour myself out for souls. I recalled the days from my youth when I told my mother over and over: "If I were a priest, I should wish to win many souls to God."[35] I had arrived at my destination, and it was time to work.

Right away, it was my parents' examples of fortitude that kept me from sleeping in. I could have dined on meats and cheeses, rationalized away meditative prayer, and given into many of Satan's temptations toward comfort. Without their example, I could have become lost in the wilds of lust or fallen into overly chummy relationships with townsfolk. Without vigilance to please God throughout the day, I may have chosen to absolve sin for just a few hours a week. I suspected that if I had softened early on, even in my first few weeks in Ars, that I would have continued to soften—and many thousands of French souls now in heaven would have gone to hell instead because I chose the path of comfort and sloth. It has been said that I converted more than eighty thousand souls. Without suppressing the base desires of my lower nature, I would have saved—perhaps—just a few. I have

34. Donald R. Fantz, "Saint Jean-Marie-Batiste Vianney," The Angelus Online, https://isidore.co/misc/Res%20pro%20Deo/Pope%20St.%20Pius%20X%20&%E2%81%84or%20SSPX/The%20Angelus/HTMLs/236.html.

35. Lopez.

God and the witness of my parents' resolve and grit to thank for my priesthood.

Dear friends, it was because of fortitude that I spent three-quarters of my life in a confessional. I knew the long lines of unknown souls sought a shepherd with wisdom and mercy, but also one who was willing to surrender his time, and even his life, for them. Those many thousands of hours in my confessional were just another way of nailing myself closer to my suffering Savior. I preached to my flock of this type of fortitude:

> "O my children! What an example of humiliation does the good Jesus give us! Behold Him on the Cross to which our sins have fastened Him; behold Him: He calls us, and says to us, 'Come to Me, and learn of Me, because I am meek and humble of heart.'"[36]

Lastly, dear reader, never forget that your children quietly hunger for you to shepherd their souls and to work to nail your lazy tendencies to the Cross so that Jesus can be seen blooming in you by your children, family members, friends, and neighbors. The best way to steer them through these perilous times is to distance yourself from what your conscience tells you are acceptable distractions. Gossip, lazy habits, unhealthy attachments (doom scrolling in all its

36. St. John Vianney, "St. John Vianney on Pride."

forms), will need to be eliminated to shepherd the people you love—and your own souls—in these days. When you work each day to carve away at your predominant fault, you will begin to see these tendencies peel away. Thereafter, small bonfires of strength and resiliency will grow in you. This is the Fire of the Spirit, forging in you a martyrdom-to-self that will enable proper guardianship of your children and loved ones as you work to lead them to everlasting joy.

But lastly, I must warn you. There will be days when you feel sapped of energy. Still, during these tough days, I beg you to work to make holy choices for those you love. I remember in Ars always thinking: *It's better to wear out than to rust out.* Perhaps bring to mind my little statue of Mary that always managed to nudge me to fortitude in doing the hard thing. Also, if your child has wandered from the Faith, remember that your distress can never overshadow your parental responsibility to continue to fight for your loved lost one. God's will includes that you give everything you have to walk to Golgotha for your child, as Mary did for her Son.

After all, the good Lord seeks the good, not your earthly happiness.

A Thought on Fortitude

I once preached in a sermon: "Why not love our crosses, and make use of them to take us to heaven?"[37] *I do not recall a day in Ars when I didn't have to fight my lower nature in choosing to carry the hundreds of crosses God had allotted me that day.*

- Meditate upon the story of Christ in Matthew 4:1–11.
- Are there places in your life where you give in and quit too easily, or is there a place in you where Satan has gained a foothold? Implore God to alert you to practical ways to eliminate the devil's power; then strive—hour by hour if necessary—to detach from Satan's barnacle.
- Why do you think fortitude, or courageous endurance, is difficult to live out in these places in your life? In what ways can you imitate Christ in the desert in order to act with more fortitude to overcome your weak spots?
- Ask the Holy Spirit to strengthen and convert you, so these places of weakness become converted to fortified places of grace and virtue.

37. St. John Vianney, "To Love the Cross," *The Marian Room*, August 6, 2021, https://themarianroom.com/to-love-the-cross/.

Vianney's bedroom, full of books. Although claimed by some to be backwards or dumb, Vianney filled his mind with great theology and the lives of the saints.

Chapter 6

The Mortification of My Priesthood

(The Grace of Penance)

Some Church historians, seminary rectors, and clergy have characterized my priesthood as severe, unloving, and even harmful. Many, too, have branded the manner of my priesthood as masochistic. Is it any wonder, dear reader, why you seldom hear the mention of my name in the sermons and instruction of clergy, even though I am their patron? The prevailing view today, however, is that my approach to shepherding is antiquated and irrelevant by modern pastoral standards.

Although Popes John XXIII, John Paul II, and Benedict XVI wrote letters about my priesthood to remind clergy of the essential truth that souls are saved through a pastoral heart, I would likely be "canceled" today. Why? For the reasons I've already mentioned, of course, but also because some Church scholars argue that my priesthood was deeply influenced by Jansenism—the heresy of clerical rigorism that plagued Western Europe and France in the eighteenth century. Misguided Jansenist priests became unwitting agents of destruction. Sweeping through rural parishes and distorting the consciences of the faithful, they burdened their people with the false belief that they were doomed to live under the unbreakable yoke of their moral failings. This cruel lie sparked fires of scrupulosity among the laity, convincing them that their depravity left them powerless to control their will. In time, some laity even welcomed macabre tortures—verbal abuse, scourgings, beatings, and even crucifixions—as a means to bring them closer to Christ's "reluctantly" merciful heart and to pull them from hell.

Fariens, a town just seven kilometers northwest of Ars, became a breeding ground for this toxic influence, so much so that my bishop considered transferring me there to undo the damage. He believed the laity needed a spiritual father who could show them the love of God my flock had come to experience through my priesthood in

Ars. However, just before my transfer, the bishop changed his mind, citing the thousands of people boarding trains, hitching horses to wagons, and embarking on pilgrimages to Ars to seek absolution in my confessional.

If my bishop understood the depth of my love for souls, why do some members of the modern clergy still associate my priesthood with heretical and loveless figures? Dear reader, the reasons are many and will only be fully revealed in paradise, but I will mention two which Philomena helped me to see:

1. Because Ars's spiritual malaise led to great sin, I preached principally and unapologetically on morality. I know my warning of hell rang harshly in sinners' ears. Perhaps it seemed to them that I was proclaiming truth through the sword, but I loved them as Christ loved them. Christ did not die for men and women to be damned, so I tirelessly proclaimed the ways to heaven. I have no quarrel with historians claiming I was a Jeremiah-like figure early in my priesthood, warning parents that their ambivalence to their young adult children's behavior had imperiled both their offspring's souls and their own.

2. Because I loved my wayward flock, I crucified myself to the allure of worldly comforts and willingly afflicted my body as a ransom for their souls. I embraced a

> lifetime of mortifications, offering them as sacrifices to bring every soul in Ars closer to heaven. These acts of penance and self-denial have been undervalued by many of today's clergy. Nevertheless, it was through them—through this love in action—that Ars was transformed and grace poured out upon the souls entrusted to my care.

Once, a parish priest came to me lamenting the indifference of his people and the seeming fruitlessness of his work. I replied in words that both angered and startled him, but later led to a humiliating awareness of his lukewarm pastoral care.

> "You have preached, you have prayed; but have you fasted? Have you taken the discipline? Have you slept on the bare floor? So long as you have done none of these things you have no right to complain."[38]

Today's clergy may be similarly bewildered by the spiritual sloth of their parishioners, but if they refuse to engage the difficult cross of penance, they should not be surprised. Some of these priests are the very ones who view me as a priest of extremes, one who ascended to the furthest edge of recklessness—flogging, assaulting, and mutilating myself—only to waste away in a frail

38. Conlin.

and broken husk of a body. But in truth, I was nothing more than a simple priest with a supernatural faith. I merely sought to follow Christ's own words in my efforts to lead the grace-starved souls of Ars to paradise. "This kind cannot be driven out by anything but prayer and fasting," Jesus said of an intractable demon in Mark 9:29. The cost of casting out demons, as Christ himself taught, was nothing less than the embrace of the Cross. I often told my flock in Ars: "Our greatest cross is the fear of crosses."[39]

Ah, if today's priests could eavesdrop on the conversations that crackle in heaven when the anchorites, hermits, and ascetics gather to tell the hidden stories of their lives—and how the annihilation of their comforts brought parishes, towns, and entire countrysides back to God. Each of these warrior-saints battled with Satan for souls. Margaret of Cortona, Anthony of the Desert, Paul the Hermit, Clare and the Poor Man of Assisi, the Stylite, Damian, and the many other dry martyrs knew the embrace of victimhood was the cost of resembling the Victim hanging from the cross. These white martyrs knew that Christ, too, was sand whipped, famished, wearied, and lonesome when he overcame the devil before beginning his ministry. Because of humanity's sin,

39. Taylor Engel, "19 Inspiring Quotes from St. John Vianney," *The Catechism Guy*, https://thecatechismguy.com/quotes-from-st-john-vianney/.

the ascetics remained steadfast in their mission, offering themselves as a ransom to overcome the power of evil and to save souls. In their humility, these stunning saints understood that they, too, needed to embrace penances to confront and overcome their own sin. And as they died to themselves, the people in the surrounding towns and villages began to grow in holiness.

My dear parents and grandparents, siblings, friends, and neighbors, it is the same for you today. You too must seek ways to begin shedding your comforts, so that you might bring solace to the lost souls within your own families. If you are already making sacrifices for them, I urge you to consider deepening these acts of love for their sake. In his beneficence and mercy, God often will use these very self-denials to bring your suffering ones back to him. Why does he work this way? When you unite penance with your prayers, God sees a reflection of his Son, who became the suffering servant to save us. Just as Christ redeemed the world through the agony he endured, he will use your acts of penance and love to lift up those for whom you intercede.

A life without self-denial rejects the example of Jesus, the Poor Man of Nazareth, who had no place to lay his head. Comfort endangers the soul because it fosters a lukewarm spirit—a spirit that, as God warned, he will spew from his mouth on the day of judgment (see Rv 3:16). I warned the hardworking farmers of Ars about the peril to their eternal souls when they sought refuge in taverns after a long day's work, instead of retreating to the warmth of their homes and the heart of their families. Why, then, do you not deny yourself the fleeting pleasure of what you consider a well-earned beer or whiskey, rather than embracing your true calling as the shepherd of your home?

I preached strongly to these men in sermons:

> Poor blind creature, who gives one hand to God and the other to the world. . . .
>
> . . . The lukewarm soul comes to the point of being completely indifferent to its own loss. It has nothing left but a love without tenderness, without action, and without energy which sustains it with difficulty in all that is essential for salvation. . . .
>
> . . . In the morning it is not God who occupies his thoughts, nor the salvation of his poor soul; he is quite taken up with thoughts of work. His mind is so wrapped up in the things of earth that the thought of God has no place in it. He is thinking about what he is going to be doing during the day, where he will be sending his children and his various employees, in what way he will expedite his own work. To say his prayers, he gets down on his knees, undoubtedly, but he does not know what he wants to ask God, nor what he needs, nor even before whom he is kneeling. His careless demeanor

> shows this very clearly. It is a poor man indeed who, however miserable he is, wants nothing at all and loves his poverty. It is surely a desperately sick person who scorns doctors and remedies and clings to his infirmities.[40]

Because over the past half century many of today's clergy and formators have diminished the supernatural value of fasts, penances, denials, and corporal mortifications, I cannot blame you for asking: *Why, Curé, such a rigorous way? Isn't prayer, charity, example, and good will enough?* I will answer in the simplest way I know: Despite many priests' apparent aversion to the Cross, sacrifice is the demand of their priesthood. Paul explained in the Letter to the Hebrews:

> For every high priest chosen from among men is appointed to act on behalf of men in relation to God, to offer gifts and sacrifices for sins. He can deal gently with the ignorant and wayward, since he himself is beset with weakness. Because of this he is bound to offer sacrifice for his own sins as well as for those of the people. (5:1–3)

But dear reader, it's my testimony that this type of sacrifice is also demanded of you in your share of the common priesthood. But since God has asked me to coach you—and

40. St. John Vianney, *The Sermons of the Curé of Ars*, trans. Una Morrissy (Roman Catholic Books, 1959), pp. 1, 6, 7.

not impose or command—I will share the story of how I came to know that my embrace of penances helped to steal souls from Grappin.

From my earliest days in Ars, Grappin mocked the efficacy of the grace conferred by my office—and, in a real sense, I understood why. The few penitents who came to my confessional often fell back into their sinful ways. Ars's decline in faith had bred a spiritual rootlessness and aridity. The concupiscence within the souls of my penitents had become hardened, and their hearts seemed impervious to grace. Grappin understood that their ability to access God's sanctification had been hindered by unbreakable patterns of sin. When he saw my discouragement in absolving the same mortal sins time and again, he never let up. He cackled and spit on my hand of absolution, calling it nothing more than an ancient lie of Catholicism—another piece of worthless, ancient folklore.

Day after day, I begged God for the wisdom to know how to stem the tide of sin that had overtaken Ars. I longed to sanctify these poor souls, but I knew that as long as they remained enslaved to their sinful habits, Grappin would relentlessly tighten his grip on them. Then, one day in prayer, a thought came: If I was going to urge them to fight their sin, it was my duty as their shepherd to enter into their trench and work right alongside them. I realized then, *Lord, I cannot tame their sins, but I can do more to help carve them out. Make me a weapon for their sake.*

From that moment, I took to heart Christ's reminder of how fasting cast out the demon from the epileptic[41] boy and began to intensify my various forms of self-denial. In the spiritual war to lead the wayward souls of Ars back to the bosom of Christ, I knew I had to rebel against myself—and against Grappin—by crucifying my "cadaver" to the crosses of my penitents' sins. To shepherd Ars effectively, I had to offer my own body with Christ's as a holocaust, a sacrifice in atonement for their souls.

Despite my increasing fasts and penances, Ars's spiritual lethargy persisted. My life of prayer, preaching, instruction, and charity would stir their souls, but I realized that the renunciation of my own body might become the greatest unseen gift I could offer them. So, I expanded and intensified my self-denials, offering every inch of my meager five-foot-one-inch frame as expiation. I had nailed the ignorance of my flock's fate to the wood of the Cross; I just needed to wait on God to work in them. In time, a few souls in Ars began to shed the weight

41. See Matthew 17:15. This is the essentially same account as Mark 9:29, with variations: The Gospel of Matthew describes the boy as a "lunatic" or "epileptic," while the Gospel of Mark consistently recounts that Jesus spoke of prayer and fasting as the only remedy for such demons. Most scholars believe that Matthew 17:21, in which Jesus speaks of prayer and fasting and which is omitted in many Bibles today, was a scribe's mistake and was not included in the earliest versions of the Gospel of Matthew.

of their sins. They were awakening, in part, because I took the greater burden of their penances upon myself in confession, leaving them only a small portion to bear.

This is what my self-denial for the souls of Ars resembled: I often slept in my presbytery attic and kitchen, and on the floors of barns, where I used an oversized brick as a pillow. When I slept in my bedroom, I removed handfuls of hay from my mattress to make sleep less comfortable. I ate sparingly and often went without meals for a few days at a time. When I did eat, my menu consisted of cold potatoes and a burnt flour snack called *matefaim*. To join myself to the physical suffering Christ endured, I lashed my left shoulder blade each night with a knotted cord. I prayed the Rosary in the sleet, rain, and snow, often holding my arms cruciform as a way of lifting Ars's souls to God. I sold every good—and every gift that came my way—to deprive myself in the fashion of the Poor Man on the Cross. I spent many thousands of frigid wintertime hours absolving sin. In the summer months, my confessional became like a tight coffin fit to faint in. Penitents never knew my trick to stay alert: I wore a hairshirt beneath my cassock. Around my upper arms were bracelets of iron bands that bristled with barbed edges.

Jesus, of course, embraced violence to redeem humanity—and Fr. Balley taught me that I could become like Christ only when I actually *became* Christ. Because I desired to resemble him in every dimension, I wanted to lift the souls of Ars as he showed me in the Gospels. Because Christ knelt alone in Gethsemane, I often knelt entire nights in prayer. Because Christ was starved of sleep from the Last Supper until his death, I usually slept no more than a few hours each night. The blood that flecked my bedroom walls was Christ's own at his scourging. Because Christ was crowned, I wore sharp-tipped bracelets and taut chains around my torso. As he carried the weight of his Cross, I would carry the weight of penitents' sins. The discomfort of my numberless hours in my cramped confessional was simply an attempt to imitate his own immobilization to the wood of his Cross. My shaky arms, outstretched for extended periods in prayer, were his, spread from east to west in agony and supplication.

As I merged these mortifications with the penances I gave to the few parishioners who trickled into my confessional, I didn't realize what God had prepared in me. In my fight against Grappin for souls, I had unwittingly managed to master my body and emotions for the hundreds of thousands of penitents who would eventually travel many miles to my confessional. My invisible war for the souls of a few hundred farmers in Ars would spread to all of France, other parts of Europe, and even into cities and towns in the Americas, whose citizenry boarded ships to kneel before my absolving hand. As I fought for Ars, my body, mind, and soul were being set right, prepared for my seemingly never-ending fourteen-hour days in the confessional. I didn't shrink from those long hours, though, because I had learned how to nail my cadaver to the wood of Christ's Cross, to remain where he poured his saving blood into my soul.

Dear friends, I again urge you in your common priesthood to begin to offer yourselves up for your loved ones. Your sacrifices and shaving of comforts are acts of love that often strike the match and illuminate the path for your lost loved one to travel back. Your penances carry enormous supernatural weight because they reflect the manner of Christ in his passion.

It is important to remember that when Jesus summoned the twelve and gave them power and authority over demons and diseases, he sent them out with nothing. No apostle had a walking stick, food, money, or a second tunic. It would be their scarcity of provisions that would heighten and effectuate their mission to proclaim the kingdom of God; comfort, Jesus knew, would just taint and blunt it.

It is the same for you. You will find your sanctity lessening when you allow yourself to be pulled to excessive measures of luxury and leisure. An unbalanced immersion in the comforts of the world will almost always pull your eyes off your duty to protect the lost loved ones in your life. Inversely, though, when you begin to commit to self-denials for the sake of your loved ones, you will see a magnificent phenomenon begin to unfold. As you detach from the world, you will often see the recipients of your sacrifices detaching from the world as well. As you decrease, these souls will seem to increase in their return to God.

A second stunning dynamic will also unfold when you embrace penances for your loved ones—you will notice your worries lessening. This is because your sacrifices have harmonized your mind, body, and soul to fully surrender to God's providence as he goes about his work to respond to your pleas. God's grace is perfecting your nature; he is working to tame your natural temptation to worry and replacing it with faith in his paternal goodness. In a sense, your sacrifices will be your "skin in the game." They will bring light to your loved ones as you fasten tightly to Christ's call in Luke 9:23: "If anyone wishes to come after me, he must deny himself and take up his cross daily." Your prayer coupled with this purgative way is the greatest method and spiritual weapon in your fight for those who are lost.

Importantly, I want you to consider one last type of self-emptying. I once described it this way: "The good

God does not require of us the martyrdom of the body; he requires only the martyrdom of the heart and of the will."[42] What is this *martyrdom of the heart and will?* Because I wasn't a great thinker, I was forced to simplify everything in my life. I realized that life consisted of making hundreds of choices each day; I could either choose the path of the saints or the wide and easy path of the world. Here lies the sacred secret of your penances: Very rarely will you desire to fast, avoid sweets, take a cold shower, deprive yourself of a few hours of sleep, or subtract from any other material comfort. It is part of your DNA, as it was mine, to avoid discomfort. But you will learn to master your heart and will when you recall that Christ, in his humanity, was also faced with countless unwanted choices each day—*the choices he made for you.* He patiently endured his enemies, poverty, sleepless nights, and faintheartedness from his closest friends *for love of you.* He desires that you love in the same dimension. It will be through your daily series of choices, your willingness to accept a diminishment of self, that your lost ones will see. Perhaps the penultimate example of this is the centurion, who marveled at the Slaughtered Lamb on the Cross, and then came to know he was God. The witness of your loving sacrifices will help

42. Engel.

to convert your children and—little by little—the world in exactly the same fashion.

Lastly, if you are unaccustomed to obtaining graces for loved ones through penances, read from the lives of the saints as often as you are able. The saints' varying stories of heroism will paint portraits of exceptionalism in your pursuit for holiness. Because they mortified their lives and stripped themselves of all comforts to become aligned with the crucified Christ, millions of souls were saved.

I once said: "The good God looks at neither long nor beautiful prayers, but at those that come from the bottom of the heart."[43] Your uneaten cupcake, the elimination of scrolling, lukewarm showers, and skipped meals are acts of love "from the bottom of the heart." It is only when you begin to detach from your comforts that you will truly enter the trenches alongside your loved ones. And in those moments, God will enter with you.

A Thought on Penance

I once preached, "How sweet it is to die if one has lived on the Cross!"[44] *In your world, sweetness from "living on the cross" makes little sense. But consolations do come from an embrace of the Cross. The daily practice of self-denial crucifies*

43. Patricia Mitchell, "Saint of the Confessional," *The Word Among Us*, https://wau.org/resources/article/saint_of_the_confessional/.

44. Fr. Roger Landry, "Death and Glory," *Mary Foundation*, June 11, 2010, https://www.catholicity.com/commentary/landry/00856.html.

the concupiscence of the flesh and helps to fashion the will to please God alone.

- Meditate upon Christ's words in Mark 12:41–44.
- Do you struggle with the discomfort that penance brings, or the desire for instant gratification over the grace that comes from mortifying oneself?
- Giving our time in prayer, our physical comfort in fasting, and our worldly comfort in almsgiving creates a discomfort that fortifies our spirits; what are ways in which you can create a better culture of penance in your home and in your life?
- Consider what motivates you to embrace the Cross on a deeper level daily and ask the Lord to accompany you, encourage you, and strengthen you in these daily moments.

The body of St. John Vianney, enshrined above the main altar in the Basilica of Ars. The Basilica is placed under the patronage of St. Philomena, and it forms an extension to the old church, the parish church of Saint-Sixte.

Chapter 7

The Penetrating Effect of Greatness of Soul

(Your Magnanimity Brings Hearts to Conversion)

Many forget that I was raised to be a farmer. For years, my father placed me in fields beside quiet men with cracked hands—grain and vineyard farmers, cattlemen, potato harvesters, deer hunters, and the like—who on Sunday left their pitchforks and sheaves and dropped to their knees to begin long strings of prayers before Mass. I didn't know their inner hearts. But in heaven, I've come to know their prayers were a commingling of countless farming worries—supplications for resilience, for rain, for an end to blight, for a sick calf to make it through the night, in thanksgiving for a harvest, and on and on. Before receiving Christ's Flesh on their tongues, these farmers begged for his mercy. They knew they often allowed their worries to disturb their attention in the Mass, just as they sometimes crept into the decades of the family Rosary. Often, thoughts of their fields overshadowed their responsibility to love their wives as they deserved. While the farmers of Dardilly worked hard to feed their families, they also recognized their deeper role as caretakers of their families' souls. So, at the end of another day in the field, they laughed with their children, captivated their souls with stories of the saints, and prayed at their bedsides before sharing a cup of tea with their wives before sleep. Then, well before the break of dawn, they worked, becoming like Christ at Golgotha. Keeping their heads down for sixteen or seventeen hours, they moved forward, obliging their burden and identity.

There was no faking it in my village. Only an embrace of total sacrifice would do. Farmers earned their pay by carrying an unsentimental clarity of what was expected of them; weariness, lonesomeness, and a sore body meant nothing under harvest moons with winter closing in. But when these farmers tried each day to resemble the Victim on the Cross, they knew they had a shot at it and that their farm might make it another year. Sacrifice was the demand of their identity, so they kept working until they no longer could.

Dear reader, it was in these graced farmlands that the mysteries of my identity were forged, until one day it became fully revealed in Ars. The witness of these big-hearted men gave birth to what became perhaps my most vital virtue as a curé. God revealed to me after my death that I was a *magnanimous* priest. For forty-one years I saw Ars as wide-open farmland, and strove each day to bring harvests of perfected souls to God. From the outset of my priesthood, I felt that generosity of heart and the desire to do great things for God would ultimately prevail in winning souls for him.

Since the term *magnanimity* is rarely used in your day, I'll shovel down to its root. The term comes from the Latin words *magnus,* meaning "great," and *animus,* meaning "spirit." As a priest, I knew magnanimity meant working to become "great-souled" or "big-hearted" for Ars. Although, dear reader, you too should strive to please God through your greatness of soul, priests uniquely understand how the virtue of magnanimity aligns with Christ. He modeled for them nobility of character, courage, generosity, inner joy, sacrificial love—and even perfection. Pope Benedict XVI described a magnanimous soul when he said: "The ways of the Lord are not comfortable. But we were not created for comfort, but for greatness."[45]

Today, as you hold my letter, does your life resemble the farmers of Dardilly who wanted to give all they had to God and their family? As you step from your bedside in the morning, is your first thought to speak words of love to your Almighty Father? *Lord thank you for a restful sleep. Lift my mind now to your desires, and grant this unworthy servant the graces necessary to fully give you my prayers, joys, works and sufferings today—so that I might share your divine love to the souls you place before me today. Gloria Patri, et Filio, et Spiritui Sancto.*

These were the predawn whisperings I often overheard from my father, who toiled relentlessly every day of his life. Despite weariness from long days managing the family farm, he strove to carry his magnanimous heart back to his wife and his children when he walked into his home after sunset. He and the ever-patient Fr. Balley were as big-hearted as anyone I knew. I pray you strive each day for greatness of soul, because your witness of magnanimity is one of the most important virtues today. Although there remain many good-willed souls in your society, an infestation of mean-spiritedness, selfishness, and pettiness

45. Edward P. Sri, "Called to Greatness: The Virtue of Magnanimity," *Lay Witness* (November/December 2009), Catholic Education Resource Center, https://catholiceducation.org/en/education/called-to-greatness-the-virtue-of-magnanimity.html.

grows like ever-expanding weeds. Modern technology, the frantic pace of life, cultural homogenization, and a pulling away from faith has poured anger, vindictiveness, unruly emotions, and unseen woundedness into every corner of your world. Many have left God behind; they do not understand his burning love for them. This is what I encountered in Ars.

Permit me to show you how I scattered the first seeds of magnanimity, and how the slow resurrection of Ars began. With no fanfare, from my earliest days in Ars, I tried to love my parishioners as Christ did from the Cross. Although I sacrificed, prayed, and catechized souls in Ars, I knew my people's minds were mostly on their crops. So, I joined the farmers in their fields and offered my help. I didn't know how this small act of generosity would act as the catalyst that softened their hearts. All these years later, these once unchurched or fallen-away Catholic farmers will tell you that it was their sweat-stained and cassocked pastor pulling potatoes beside them that led them back to the sacraments. I've come to realize that the magnanimity of my round-the-clock availability in the confessional helped revive an entire countryside—and much of a nation—choked by the aftermath of the French Revolution.

But first, it must be mentioned: Very few believed the conversion of Ars would happen. The souls of this village of forsaken people had been methodically garroted by wars, isolation, and fatherlessness. The destabilization had turned Ars into a lonely land of farmers who shifted their once-fervent devotion to God to the fickle god of the crops in their back field. Rather than falling to their knees like the farmers of Dardilly to plead for God's divine hand to end a blight, they shook their fists at heaven to curse God and their fate. When I considered what their self-inflicted sacramental famine had blinded them to—the drought in their own hearts—I knew I had my work cut out. Most of them didn't trust or even like men in cassocks.

As I mentioned, the bleakness of the times caused a few of Ars's previous pastors to leave the priesthood altogether. The question must be asked (I certainly asked it privately then): Why would once-willing priests divorce themselves from their flock and flee their obligatory rescue mission? I have come to know that these priests quit after considering the amount of pastoral labor required to revitalize what they saw as an impossibly unholy backwater. Ars wasn't unconquerable, though; it was simply a community starved of love, a village in which 280 souls could one day become saints.

I began visiting every home in Ars, working to soften my parishioners' antagonism and show them my heart. When I wasn't praying and fasting for them, I continued to work with them on their farms. As their new shepherd, I knew the best way to break through the hard scabs of their cynicism was to *become one of them* and share in their toil. Some farmers, who quietly marveled at my generosity, invited me to their humble harvest festivals. A few others welcomed me into their homes for meals. When they did, I took the opportunity to share my father's farming secrets and the memories of tending the fields of Dardilly. If I sensed the mood of the evening becoming merry and light, I spoke of the everlasting love and mercy God had for them—then invited them to return to Mass. They often looked down to the floor when I told them I had grown weary of St. Sixtus feeling lonelier than Gethsemane.

Still, the farmers and their families kept to their fields on Sundays. But since I had established friendships with them, I kept visiting them in their fields. They didn't know I was working strenuously to turn over and till the hard soil of their hearts. With a blood loyalty to my identity as a spiritual farmer, I knew I had to shovel deep to clear out all the moles, earwigs, and other critters that had snaked into their souls and caused them to forsake God and the sacraments. Until their spiritual weeds were torn away and uprooted, I knew that any seeds I scattered were unlikely to take root.

When a few farmers and their families returned to Mass, I knew Grappin would work to bring them straight back to the god of their field. Because he posed a danger to their budding desire for holiness, I built barricades of pastoral protection around them. These prayers, fasts, and self-denials were like immovable rings of iron. In the privacy of my presbytery and parish, I goaded Grappin to bring his attacks against me alone, which he of course did.

More and more farmers invited me into their homes after days in their fields. When I engaged them and asked why they no longer received the sacraments, I listened patiently to their excuses without letting them know they had stepped on a third rail. These farmers, I knew, found time to fill their emptiness with ale and whiskey at the taverns, but never thought of inebriating their souls with the Blood of Christ. Because I knew these hardy men appreciated candor, I spoke hard things to them about the condition of their souls, explaining that even though they were humble and hardworking, a life without God would likely eternally damn their souls to hell. When they saw my rebukes always joined with my tears, they knew I loved them and their families. Even better, they saw that I deeply loved their souls, and wanted to trellis them toward heaven.

I often smile when Ars is remembered as a country hamlet filled with holy and hardy souls. Ars was not converted with a few sweeps of a wand; it required time, patience, and great effort to remain stouthearted for my people. It took eight years for most of Ars's fallen-away faithful to come back to Sunday Mass; ten years to convince them to confess their sins; twenty years for the pilgrimages to Ars to begin; twenty-five years to close down the taverns; and thirty years to eliminate the cabarets that had led to the late-night lust. Through God's grace and his divine aid, by the time of my death Ars had become a countryside of willing saints.

All the while, I did not realize it was the virtue of magnanimity that helped turn Ars around. I attributed all the graces and miracles to the intercession of my martyr-friend, Philomena. To be honest, I didn't even know what magnanimity meant until my judgment, when the Savior spoke the word as he welcomed me into paradise. He explained how my relentless efforts to save the souls of Ars had brought great joy to his Father and to all of heaven. Then, with a warm smile, Philomena said: *Well done, Jean-Marie. The red martyrs and I have been waiting for you; you've shown them something nobler than the way we died. Through your embrace of dry martyrdom, you've allowed them to marvel at a lifetime of magnanimous love.*

Just as magnanimity was the key to eradicating the spiritual blight in Ars, so too will it be through your magnanimous actions that the moral disorder of the West can be restored to grace and order. The truest measure of my love for souls was how much of myself I poured out for them. The same is true for you.

As you read this sentence, it is likely that souls are suffering within walking distance from your doorstep. Your world has become choked with lonely souls. Many of them are your neighbors; they are the prodigal sons and daughters you walk and drive past and wave to each day. They are the brokenhearted ones who have forgotten—or simply do not know—that a Father loves them and awaits their return. A jeweled ring, a killing of the fatted calf, and a long and tender embrace await. But these gifts of homecoming are just the "day one" offerings of the Father's measureless love; he has so much more in store for these lost lambs.

Dearest reader, in these increasingly godless days of reengineered moral norms and annihilation of the ordered ways I once knew in Dardilly, you must pour out your magnanimous heart, liked a tipped-over chalice of the Lord's most precious Blood. Until these wandering souls see you at their doorstep with an invitation to share a meal, they can't begin to know the Father's love through your own demonstration of care for their souls.

Entire hospitals, barb-wired prisons, and the floors of eerily quiet retirement homes and assisted living centers ache for magnanimous hearts. But so does your neighbor who, unlike those in the aforementioned places, appears to be content—even happy—and comfortable as he or she lives out the "American Dream." But if this soul does not know God—or has rejected him for the world—you, reader, must go to his or her doorstep. Your knocking hand serves as the hand of Jesus Christ.

And after your neighbor opens the door and the Holy Spirit begins to speak, you must know that your neighbor will see something as uncommon as it is transcendent: he will see the beating of your magnanimous heart.

A Thought on Magnanimity

The spirit of magnanimity leads to a fearlessness in preaching the gospel and witnessing to truth, even when it's difficult. If through my big-heartedness I managed to convert a town and much of a nation, I imagine you can do much to convert a family member or a friend.

- Meditate upon Christ's words and actions in Luke 4:16–30.

- Christ's magnanimity exuded from his every word and deed. In what ways do you have a magnanimous spirit? In what ways are you lacking?

- How you can extend yourself to love someone who has fallen away, back into the embrace and safety of the Church?
- Ask the Lord to give you opportunities for evangelization, courage to step up to the task and be his witness, and magnanimity of spirit to face whatever the consequences of speaking and living the truth.

"Apparition de sainte Philomène au curé d'Ars" is a delicate stained-glass window design by 19th-century workshop Gsell-Laurent, depicting St. Philomena appearing to Vianney, renowned for his devotion to her. This artwork reflects both the rich artistic heritage of ecclesiastical glassmaking of the period, and France's deep devotion to Vianney, who won over the hearts of his countrymen through his white martyrdom of asceticism and dedication to the salvation of their souls. Detail, ink and watercolor on tracing paper.

Chapter 8

How to Achieve Sanctity

(God's Divinization Begins with a Trickle)

You've neared the end of my letter to you, and with it, the only question that truly matters to God in the end: Did you strive to love like Christ and to live a life of holiness? Or, to put it another way—did you love the Lord your God with all your heart, soul, mind, and strength? Striving for holiness should be your identity, God's presence within you, the mark of your soul that fills you, that makes you like a chalice meant to be tipped over and poured out for humankind.

Saints make saints. The light of God's very self, living within you, will help your children—or family members, friends, and neighbors—to become holy. And if your children have left the Faith, it will be your unwavering commitment to God and pursuit of holiness that will help to bring them back.

But what exactly is holiness, and why has it become difficult for so many to attain? In fairness, there are no Palestinian caves with hidden scrolls containing the secret of sanctity. The tales of long-dead saints and hermits might pour like polyphony into your soul, but they will not make you holy. Your most singular inspiration or theologically opulent thought to please God might emerge later today, but unless you dispose yourself to seeing it through, you will not be suddenly holy and may even find yourself less so.

Dear reader, the secret to a life of deep spiritual intimacy with God is simple and straightforward: Begin to beg God to move your impulse to do good from your head to your will. Beseech the Lord to transform your motive for *doing* good as much as you beg him to *think* of good things. As your coach, I urge you to write this plea on a slip of paper—*Loving Father, help me to move my desire for holiness to my will.* Perhaps fasten these words to your bathroom mirror or strive to make them a type of first commandment ordered to please God. In time, if you consistently begin to transfer your desire to do good *to actually doing what is good*, you will be well down the path of profound spiritual union with God. Why is this?

Because you will have surrendered your senses, will, and flawed human tendencies to him.

The Church, in her maternal wisdom, has not declared me one of her doctors. Still, as one of her canonized saints and the patron of parish priests, I do know the sure path to holiness—and for a single reason: I want to lead you to it. God hungers for you to be holy. He longs for deep and personal union with you. A note on your mirror is a good reminder of how holiness is achieved, but until you see how God plays his part, you might not believe that a life of sanctity is possible for you. But it is, and as your coach, I will show you why.

I mentioned the name Abbé François Trochu earlier, for good reason. Of the many biographers who've worked to describe my essence, no man explored more deeply my work, nature, habits, and heart. So penetrating was Fr. Trochu that he was able to describe the actual state and appearance of my soul, which was the pure light of God. "The first glimpse of the holy man was sufficient to fill [pilgrims to Ars] with awe and admiration, for they saw how the beauty of his soul transfigured his outward appearance," Fr. Trochu wrote. "It seemed as if he were endued with extraordinary strength from Heaven. . . .

Beneath the covering of an attenuated, almost transparent body, the soul of the Curé d'Ars shone forth."[46]

Paul wrote of this type of inflowing of divine love in his Letters to the Ephesians, telling them they could "be filled with all the fullness of God" (Eph 3:19). He wanted even the earliest believers to understand the astonishing idea that the risen Christ could actually *rise in them*—or put another way, that the frailness of their humanity could become divinized. This is the physiological and deeper ontological change that Trochu explained arose in me.

What Paul told those early believers holds true for you: God so desires divine intimacy and union with you that, with your cooperation, he will infuse you—or sanctify you—with himself so that you become like him. It cannot be emphasized enough: In these days of broadening moral collapse, God begs for you to become "another Christ" and torchlight for all wandering in spiritual darkness. Your holy witness will manifest in remarkable ways when you turn from sin and open yourself to receive the foremost gift of his divine grace.

Abstract philosophical concepts like *infusion* or *divinization* were always confusing to me, so I will speak plainly about the supernatural movement of grace, and why it is necessary for you to attain holiness. Without

46. Trochu, pp. 443, 445.

this infusion of God, you will never be able to enter into the mystical marriage he so desires with you. I don't remember a time when I wasn't drawn to meditating on the life of Christ and desiring to please him. This might seem insignificant (and I imagine it did when I meditated on Christ as a small child), but in my natural exercise of considering God, he was, in a way, tenderly beginning to dissolve into me. Without my knowledge, I was being infused with his love. Essentially, the more I meditated on Jesus, even as a child, the more he beckoned me to become like him.

As time went on, I gradually began to feel God's presence concretely, as his essence trickled into me. St. Athanasius wrote jarring words before the Ecumenical Council in Nicaea in AD 325: "For the Son of God became man so that we might become God."[47] The *Catechism*, echoing these words, emphasized them with the writings of St. Peter: "The Word became flesh to make us '*partakers of the divine nature*.'"[48] I am testimony that Athanasius's words are true.

For twenty-eight years, I always considered and adored my Jesus as a loving Savior who was *out there*. But soon after my ordination, he no longer was *out there*;

47. St. Athanasius, *De inc.* 54, 3: PG 25, 192B quoted in *Catechism of the Catholic Church*, no. 460.

48. 2 Pt 1:4, quoted in *Catechism of the Catholic Church*, no. 460.

Christ began to become a part of my innermost self. As his embrace held firm and broadened, an undertow of longing to know, love, and serve God surged more deeply in me. I imagined then it was in the same dimension as the great Carmelite mystics, Teresa and John. Holiness, though, is not constrained to merely resembling a Carmelite, a mystic, or a certain saint; the shape of our holiness is unique for each of us.

Before delving deeper into the mystical movement of God's grace, it may be helpful to begin with a few foundational truths that all Catholics affirm. Because humanity needed salvation, God came to us through his Son. When we respond to his sacrificial love by loving him in return, we are transformed into his likeness through the prompting and indwelling of the Holy Spirit. The inevitable result of the Spirit's presence within us is divine light—a light that is nothing less than his very divinity.

Here is how my mystical marriage with God, in fits and starts, became perfected. As I mentioned earlier, when I came to understand the hardness of my flock's stony hearts, I began spending greater amounts of time behind the closed doors of St. Sixtus imploring God's consolation, wisdom, and strength to help save Ars. I knew the grace of my office alone wasn't enough to penetrate sin-darkened souls; I needed God to do the work in me. To become a suitable placeholder for Jesus to turn hearts inside out, I knew I needed to work to *become* him. Practically, I began to intensify my prayer; for hours at a time I drank deeply from the wells of contemplation. There were many nights when my heart overflowed with love, and I was lifted into ecstasy. But when that spiritual warmth faded, I found myself speaking to God about my fears, my struggles as a priest, and my worries for Ars. In those moments, it seemed as though God had departed. But in truth, he had gone nowhere. It was I who had pulled away, hindered by my own lack of trust in his love, guiding hand, and omnipotence. God desired that I surrender all my uncertainties and pain into the furnace of his love, just as Jesus did from the Cross. With this humbling awareness, I often beheld the Man of Sorrows—"*Ecce homo*"[49]—and begged him to strip me of the garments of my fear and crown me with his thorns. From the foot of his Cross, I implored him to tear away my doubts and fashion me into a priest abandoned completely to his care for me.

I wanted to love Jesus as I had loved him when I was an untroubled little boy, with total trust in God's care. Jesus's words in Matthew reoriented me to the priesthood he desired from me: "Truly, I say to you, unless you turn and become like children, you will never enter the kingdom of heaven" (18:3). So, I spoke in the same open-

49. "So Jesus came out, wearing the crown of thorns and the purple robe. Pilate said to them, 'Here is the man!'" (Jn 19:5).

hearted and uncomplicated manner I did while tending my father's sheep. I used small, guileless words to praise God for the grace of my priesthood. I thanked him for the worries, weight, and burden of Ars. I abandoned myself fully to him in the same way I had allowed myself to dissolve into the warmth of my mother's embrace. In a way I didn't realize then, I was loving him like Beloved John, who rested his head against Jesus's heart, with no agenda except to love him.

In the process of surrendering all to him, the trickles of transformation began to irrigate and well up within me. In the silence of those nights, everything that had always felt pure, sacred, and light when I contemplated Christ began pouring into me. As my heart brimmed over with love, he seemed to sharpen his gaze in me and point me to what he desired from my priesthood. Thereafter, I widened my sacrifices, penances, and acts of charity for the souls of Ars. In the process, I made a small discovery: Unless I willingly nailed myself to the Cross for the recovery of Ars, Christ could never fully live in Ars—or in me! If it was to be consummated, God's divinization *needed to be lived out through my surrender to him.* As I strove to live out the priesthood God demanded—and that Ars required—he seemed to have taken a spiral staircase down into the depths of my soul, and he never went back up. God was—as Athanasius wrote—divinizing me.

Thereafter, as biographers have noted, God gave me a knowledge of souls for the thousands of pilgrims who came to Ars to confess their sins. Jesus had become my essence—and yes, I will say it: In time, I had *become* Jesus. This was around the time Grappin, alas, surrendered his long fight. Before he departed, he said through the shrieking words of a possessed woman, "If there were three like you on earth, my kingdom would be destroyed."[50]

In your day, the mention of what I give testimony to—the divinization of Jesus in me—may ring as pious, preposterous, or even pridefully demonic. Modern clergy rarely speak of this efficacious operation of grace, and when it is mentioned, it is often emptied of its meaning. Because bishops and priests hardly speak of it, most Catholics worldwide don't understand their need for divinization. And those who are familiar with this mystical movement often see it as an archaic and outdated notion from the apostolic or medieval age, long past its expiration date.

But, dear reader—no. Divinization is what Christ desires to do for you! Even though your divinization might seem to be an impossibility, the Church has taught it from her beginning. Your first pope encouraged Christ's first followers—and two thousand years later, he

50. Rutler, pp. 174–175.

still encourages you—to become "partakers of the divine nature" (2 Pt 1:4). I urge you to seek this deep union with God within you, for he longs to reveal his face to the world through your life. When you open your heart to allow God to dwell in you, you will become a vessel through which many souls are led to conversion.

I never became a Trappist or had the luxury of being enfolded in the blaze of God's love. I was a parish priest with a laundry list of lukewarm souls who sorely needed a shepherd. So, I departed from St. Sixtus every morning to take part in the pastoral work I had promised God. The wonderful aspect of God's divinization that I discovered was that it is *transportable*, occurring even as I went about my priestly duties. The languorous presence of God that once seemed restricted to the catacomb-like warmth of St. Sixtus, covered me throughout even my busiest days.

In Ars, I came to see that even the smallest act of charity or pastoral care was like a snowflake gently falling onto a vast field in the French countryside. At first, I imagined God as the snow-covered field, with my acts of charity as the snowflakes that gave the meadow its blanket. But over time, I realized I had conceived of it all backward. It was God, descending from on high, and I had become his field of snow. This sacred work of divinization was his. It is why so much of France returned to the Faith after the

Revolution. And as God's graces expanded within me, so did the fruitfulness of my priesthood. God's divinization is the sweet fire of his presence that will never leave you. In fact, the fire of God will spread through your humble acts, penances, and measures of patience and kindness you allow to punctuate your days. Your loving acts become the accelerants that deepen God's presence in you.

Dear reader, this is why all of this matters: When you let go of the world, heaven becomes clearer. Unless you make a deliberate choice to ascend the heights of holiness, you will never truly become holy. You cannot hope to reverse the chaos of your time unless you decide to leave behind the Old Adam and embrace the New. If you must, picture yourself as Solomon, holding a sword in one hand and a baby in the other. A separation must occur—a decisive, clean break that opens you up to the transformative fire of God's Spirit within you. You must live in this world, but not be of it.

I had to make this cut in surrendering my feelings of inadequacy to God. In truth, this death of my insecurities had to come by a thousand cuts. God could not penetrate me unless I worked to continually slay the thoughts of my unworthiness. Of course, the people of Ars couldn't see the long and hard process of God's divinization in me, but they began to change when I finally did. My transformation into the fullness of Christ, *in persona*

Christi, cast shafts of light into their own souls. Gradually, the townsfolk saw the emptiness in their hearts and began to recognize and recoil from their sin. Though they began to change their outward habits, they knew it wasn't enough—it didn't fill the emptiness within. What they longed for was to be filled by the God they had once known—the same Spirit they saw in me, the Spirit whose penetrating love reflected in my eyes, silently pleading for them to return.

Then, the transformation began. A few tavern owners closed their businesses and a handful of farmers stopped working on Sundays. A number of the amorous twenty-something set rejected their lustful lifestyles. Some town gossips began to close their mouths. Each of them returned to the sacraments. Even a few priests who once scorned my priesthood came to me on their knees, weeping. This is what happens when a poor and willing soul asks to be divinized.

But please, dear reader—here at the end of this letter—do not regard this mysterious movement of grace as piously peculiar or unattainable for you. Each of you is capable of becoming a canonized saint, and I daresay each of you should be striving for it at this hour when the villainous serpent lurks in every shadow. (Recall St. Michael the Archangel's warning of untamed evil before he left my side.) Christ and the truth he proclaimed are gradually disappearing, like the one-by-one extinguishing of Tenebrae candles. The same questions remain.

Will you walk the path of humility I did in Ars to allow God to fully enter into your soul?

Will you intensify your prayer life, and begin each day in meditative prayer?

Will you begin to regard Mary as both ferocious and unconquerable, and implore her intercession?

Can you work to increase the virtue of fortitude, so you, too, might resemble Mary as you bring the message of her Son into a world that will often despise you?

Will you begin to mortify your emotions and your body, and work to slowly eliminate your greatest comforts so that you might be streamlined for the work God has planned for you?

Will you accept the world's rejection, the loss of friends, and even humiliation, to proclaim God?

Will you remain magnanimous when the world casts you out?

Will you continue to pursue greatness in proportion to the abilities and potential God has given you? Recall the parable of the talents, and what the master said. "For to everyone who has more will be given, and he will have abundance; but from him who has not, even what he has will be taken away" (Mt 25:29).

Will you be holy in a world that so often gnashes its teeth in a rising flood of outer darkness?

Recall your slip of paper: When *your desire* to increase your acts of love, patience, and sacrifice becomes *transferred* to your will, everything in your life will change. Things will also begin to change for the lost loved ones around you.

Like me, and all the saints in heaven, you will never become a perfected saint on earth. Even as you work to master your will through frequent acts of love and unseen sacrifices, you—like me—do not share in God's omnipotence. But your willingness to forfeit the charms of the world will allow Christ to bloom wider in you. What does this look like? Well, in Ars, seven hours of confessions doubled to fourteen. Some clergy might categorize my marathon days in the confessional as folklore—but I testify that it is true! And it was the Spirit I had allowed into me that accomplished it. God became my absolving hand, my stamina, and my burning desire to save souls. In my confessional, God himself was looking into and saving the souls of the sinners.

It was God's voice that spoke from my pulpit. How could I possibly know this? Because whereas I had once routinely spent as many as eight hours each Saturday writing down, preparing, and memorizing Sunday sermons, I mostly stopped preparing for them altogether.

When I gave way to the Spirit, many Mass-goers were held spellbound by my extemporaneous words. Even at the end, when I was toothless and my sermons were mostly inaudible, the throngs of pilgrims wept; it was the Spirit they saw and heard from my fading body I had nailed to the hard wood of Christ's own Cross.

It was God who directed my footsteps into the homes of the poor, and his words that cheered on the souls of the brokenhearted. He was the rigor behind my mortifications. And as I aged, he made my frail arms mighty when I reached for orphans, mixed the mortar, and laid the brick to help build a home for destitute girls.

And when penitents lined up to confess their sins on my deathbed, they saw my hollowed-out cheeks, pallid face, and withered body in glorious light. They saw a worn-out cadaver consumed by God's love. In my weakness, I couldn't share what the Apostle of Grace said: "It is no longer I who live, but Christ who lives in me" (Gal 2:20).

Matthew 11:12 echoes the words of Jesus: "From the days of John the Baptist until now the kingdom of heaven has suffered violence, and men of violence take it by force." They are cryptic words—but ones that ought to pierce your heart. Still, you might ask, what do Christ's peculiar words on violence have to do with the conclusion of this letter? Everything, dear reader. Everything.

I pray Christ's words take hold in the deepest part of your soul. These words speak directly to your need to fight the world's darkness and yet not be overcome by it. Jesus tells us plainly that the kingdom of heaven is not inherited passively but instead through a war against the world's darkness and a "bearing away" of one's own sin. Dear reader, he expects from you a violent insistence on his truth, on love, and on leading others to salvation. Heaven is not for the faint of heart or for those who would seek comfort; it must be seized.

I ask you now to recall the conversation of the saints that began this letter. You'll remember their candor in discussing the mourning faithful, the too-comfortable state of the Catholic Church, and the millions who risk their eternal souls by drinking from the world's poisoned chalice of sin. Remember my task—and yours. God has asked that I coach you to become the domestic priests of your homes and witnessing priests in a world that has been torn asunder by its rejection of God.

Dear reader, at this hour of growing godlessness, will you suffer violence to help save it? Didn't Christ endure violence on his Cross for you and me so that we might have life? Even as I write these words, I feel warmth entering my soul. Ah! It suddenly occurs to me that I am asking that you mimic my priesthood in Ars, to give your whole self to God alone. *Magnificat anima mea Dominum, et exultavit spiritus meus in Deo salutari meo!*[51]

Dearest priest, will you begin to live as I did in Ars, when my sacrifices, discomfiture, self-surrender, and willingness to suffer for God kindled and broadened secret fires in my soul? In time, on your most disconsolate days, you might feel your soul expand as I did. *This* is God's divinization, your transformation into the likeness of Christ. It will grow in you in proportion to your willingness to suffer violence to become a saint for the days in which you live.

The loneliness, awkwardness, fatigue, and alienation you will often feel will serve like an Angelus bell in your soul, echoing Christ's words: "If the world hates you, know that it has hated me before it hated you" (Jn 15:18). Your choice to carry Christ's Cross in a sin-darkened world, inversely, will become your greatest consolation. Your agony will become like a type of first fruit, or like the pointer finger of the Holy Ghost, urging you further up Golgotha to live and suffer as Christ.

God the Father, Philomena, and the company of priest-saints ask you now—through the imploring final words of this poor country pastor: Will you carry Christ's Cross into a world that increasingly hates its meaning? I

51. "My soul magnifies the Lord, and my spirit rejoices in God my Savior" (Lk 1:46–47).

am no longer with you in the flesh. I cannot walk beside you. But I implore you to call upon my intercession, and I will work to bring grace into your life, just as I have for the other praying souls who've reached out to me from the moment of my death. I will help you to press on through the toil—and the glory—that lies ahead.

Dear reader, as you strive to seize heaven, a most extraordinary phenomenon will unfold in you. Even after you've set your hand to the plow and are well onto your path to holiness, it is almost certain you will see yourself as a sinner still even more in need of God's grace. Years will pass and your holiness will grow. Those closest to you—your spouse, your children, your friends—and even strangers will begin to regard you as an unrecognized saint, but you won't see it. They won't know the reason for your springs of inner light, but they will *see the transformation* far more clearly than you will.

In a way they may not be able to describe, your loved ones will increasingly see you awakening each morning to scale cliff faces just to try to love them as Christ does. Handhold after handhold after handhold, they will see that you've conformed each of your choices to virtue. Few will know that the radiance of your life is actually the reflective blaze of the face of God. And of course, you won't know or care either, because you are forever in the midst of your climb.

A Thought on Divinization and Holiness

My dear friend St. Patrick once shared his prayer of complete and total self-giving to the Lord: "Christ be with me, Christ within me, Christ behind me, Christ before me, Christ beside me, Christ to win me, Christ to comfort and restore me. Christ beneath me, Christ above me. . . ."[52] *This abandonment to holiness and divinization is the perfect description of what I felt take place within my soul as the Lord allowed me to partake in his divine nature. I wish the same for you, dear reader.*

- Meditate upon the words of Christ in John 15:1–16.
- What do you think Christ means when he says, "Abide in my love"? Do you believe that the Lord has given us all the means by which to do this through his Church? Do you make use of the means the Church provides to achieve holiness? In which ways?
- The saints made frequent confession, adored Christ in the Eucharist, prayed the Rosary, and attended weekday Mass. These are the graces by which they became saints, the ones that allowed them to enter into the hardened hearts of humanity. Do you do these things? In which areas are you lacking? How can you make adjustments in order to engage in these holy practices more often?

52. "Breastplate of Saint Patrick," My Catholic Life, https://mycatholic.life/catholic-prayers/breastplate-of-saint-patrick/.

- Do you hunger for holiness? Do you strive each day to align your will and desire to God alone?
- In prayer, ask the Lord to tenderly dissolve into you, gently but surely becoming infused into your every cell. Make room for more sacraments and means of holiness in your daily life, and allow him to divinize you, because this is what he desires for you above all.
- Lastly, consider the necessity of the virtue of fortitude: When you sense this infusion taking place in you, will you actually begin to die to yourself for the lost ones? Will you die like Philomena did for Christ? Will you scale mountains for God and become the hero he desires?

Further Reading

(To Explore St. John Vianney's Life)

Miller, Frederick L. *The Grace of Ars*. Ignatius Press, 2010.

Rutler, George William. *The Curé D'Ars Today: St. John Vianney*. Ignatius Press, 1988.

de Saint Pierre, Michel. *The Remarkable Curé of Ars: The Life and Achievements of St. John Mary Vianney*. Translated by M. Angeline Bouchard. Doubleday, 1963.

Sheppard, Lancelot C. *Portrait of a Parish Priest: St. John Vianney, the Curé d'Ars*. Newman Press, 1958.

Trochu, Abbé François. *The Cure D'Ars: St. Jean-Marie-Baptiste Vianney*. TAN Books, 1977.

Vianney, St. John Marie. *The Sermons of the Curé d'Ars: For the Sundays and Feasts of the Year*. Mediatrix Press, 2016.